HIRE ON A WHIM™

A Step-by-Step Guide to Hiring Qualities That Make for Great Employees

Garrett Miller

With Contributing Writer

Jim Thrasher, Ed.D.

****

Editor

Adele Annesi

Word for Words, LLC

adeleannesi.com

On a WHIM Publishing

Second Edition 2019

First Edition 2010

Copyright © 2010 Garrett Miller

ISBN: 978-0-9826159-0-4

DEDICATION

To all those who have invested in me and continue their support
My wife, Paula
My family, friends, coaches, teachers, pastors, bosses, mentors, and readers

What Leaders Say About WHIM Now

"Hire on a WHIM is a very good book and a quick read. I believe fielding the best team is 90 percent of the job. Managers at every level must hire the right qualities in order to field the best team. WHIM will help managers succeed in this area. Garrett and Jim have done an excellent job of providing a simple framework on how to hire the right staff."

Ed Breen

CEO — TYCO

"A must-read for anyone who hires! A gem! Packed with sage advice and practical tips—this book will help you hire smart, honest, motivated winners."

Mike Song

Coauthor — The Hamster Revolution:

"With over twenty-five years of management experience at the district, regional, and national level, I have been directly involved with recruiting and hiring hundreds of candidates. The successful hires all come down to the four key facets Garrett addresses. The challenge is how to uncover the candidate's strengths and weaknesses in these areas. Garrett has provided a realistic roadmap on how to get to these issues."

Russ Gasdia

VP Sales and Marketing — Purdue Pharmaceuticals

"As an expert with over thirty-three years in organizational development, I have helped place and find top talent. WHIM is a great book for anyone who is preparing to interview for a job. Garrett helps the reader understand the qualities that today's leaders are hiring, why they ask the questions they do, and what hiring managers are listening for. I would recommend reading WHIM as part of any job search."

Charley Smith

Director of Human Capital Consulting — J.H. Cohn LLP

"The two most important skillsets for any manager are hiring the right people and developing them to be successful. Garrett Miller and Jim Thrasher do a tremendous job of bringing to life the characteristics every manager should look for when hiring. These principles are laid out in a clear and easily implemented format. Following and implementing the principles in this book will guarantee that you will build your team's foundation on solid ground."

Matt Kunzler

Director — Business Supplies and Equipment Leader

"Miller's Hire on a WHIM approach is excellent. It's very simple, yet it can have a profound positive effect on your hiring decisions. His approach addresses the non-teachable and non-negotiable personality traits that are essential for making great hires."

Larry Smith

VP Global Supply Chain — Becton Dickinson

"If you want to be an amazing recruiter, then read WHIM. Garrett and Jim's ideas are so clear, concise, and easy to understand. No matter what success I'm having as a recruiter, this book will make me better."

Chuck Sutton

Head of Recruiting — E&J Gallo and Sons

"WHIM is a great read and a must for anybody who is involved in the hiring process. My thirty-three years of hiring in some of the world's greatest and biggest companies confirm that Miller is correct; you must hire what you can't teach! I wish I had had this years ago. Now I await his next one: how to manage leaders!"

Jerry Hampton

Chairman — World Aid New York

EVP — Smith Barney, SVP — Goldman Sachs

"Terrific book. I put these principles to use the very next time I interviewed a candidate. WHIM is easy to remember, practical to apply, and essential to hire."

Michael J. Biliouris

Vice President — Salesforce

"As a true believer in the creation of highly effective teams, I see WHIM as an essential tool. Great leaders consistently surround themselves with great talent. WHIM will enable both new and experienced hiring managers to consistently identify and hire the four qualities that are vital to building a winning team culture."

Jim Edwards

President — LeaderQuest Development

CONTENTS

Forward   ix

Preface   xi

1   Another One Bites the Dust   13

Getting Started: A Self-Assessment   17

2   Laying the Foundation   18

Begin the Process   23

3   Instincts and Insights   26

Understanding Your Bias   31

4   'Listening' to the Resume   33

Prepare for the Interview   37

5   Discovering the First Quality   39

Mining the Resume   44

6   What Dose a Work Ethic Look Like?   46

Discerning a Candidate's Work Ethic   51

7   It Must Be a Fit   54

Making Sure It's a Good Fit   57

8   The Second Quality of WHIM   61

Discerning a Candidate's Integrity   67

9   Surprised   70

How Candidates Respond to Obstacles   74

10   The Third Quality   76

	Discerning a Candidate's Maturity	81
11	One More Essential Quality	83
	Discerning a Candidate's Humility	88
12	Putting the Pieces Together	92
	The Candidate Hiring Checklist	96
13	Sharon	99
	The Second Interview, Mix it Up	106
14	Brett	108
	A Better Second Interview	113
15	The Right Decision	115
	Advice on Making an Offer	119
16	Onboarding	122
	The Most Important 60 Minutes	126
17	Shoring Up the Foundation	128
	Maintaining WHIM	134
Bonus Chapter	College Recruiting	138
	Acknowledgments	147

FOREWORD

Frank Marcus
Managing Director,
Global Training & Development — E&J Gallo Winery

Building a successful organization begins with a vision, then hiring professionals to carry out that vision. Ronald Reagan said, "Surround yourself with the best people you can find, delegate authority, and don't interfere as long as the policy you've decided upon is being carried out."

Hiring the best people doesn't seem so difficult until you begin the process. Regardless of whether you're hiring for an entry-level or executive position, you must be able to identify and hire the best.

In my twenty-four years with E&J Gallo Winery and my many years in business, certain key tools have helped me work smarter. The WHIM concept is one of them. I am impressed when someone creative takes everyday life and distills it down to the basics. Myers and Briggs did that several decades ago to help us to better understand the many personalities we encounter. They took an idea that we all knew existed and gave us a simple tool with which to work smarter. Garrett Miller has accomplished this as well. In WHIM, he has given us a tool that will help every professional who hires to make better decisions.

Having excellent hiring fundamentals is essential for any organization that strives to grow and excel. It is a task that some have done well, but many have done poorly. If you have picked up this book, you already understand the high costs associated with a poor hiring decision. I hope you have also experienced the excitement of making excellent choices. In the game of staffing, "winning some and losing some" is not a profitable proposition; you must always win.

Having excellent hiring fundamentals is essential for any organization that strives to grow and excel.

I have worked both domestically and internationally, building new markets. Every success story begins with hiring the right people. However, hiring is an unforgiving process; when you make a mistake; it is costly, both personally and corporately. As the marketplace has become increasingly competitive, room for hiring errors has evaporated. This is a process that we must get right. Garrett has done a remarkable job of getting to the heart of every great hire. These are qualities I have always looked for but have never seen so clearly laid out in such a simple and understandable manner. Yes, Garrett has gotten it right—you must hire what you cannot teach. These qualities are part of a great hire's DNA.

Garrett and Jim Thrasher provide insights for anyone being hired and offer valuable concepts in applying WHIM to hiring the sometimes-unpredictable college graduate or recent graduate. I have found this population to be challenging because there is usually little in the way of work experience with which to evaluate candidates. So, what do you rely on—school pedigree, a performance review, or the candidate's latest sales numbers? Garrett and Jim help to eliminate the guesswork and give great insights on how to find and uncover the most important qualities any employee should have. They have done it in a simple and entertaining way.

During my career, I have been fortunate to have hired great people who have helped to make our company a global market leader. This is the first time I have seen these principles laid out in such a clear and easily implementable way. I have used these qualities as guidelines, whether I am hiring a new college graduate or a C-level executive. Give this book to a new hiring manager, and he is guaranteed to get it right ninety-five percent of the time.

I have used these qualities as guidelines, whether I am hiring a new college graduate or a C-level executive.

To achieve excellence, the right tools are essential. Hire on a WHIM gives you foundational and practical ways to master the art of hiring. Success may not happen on a WHIM—but hiring does.

Frank Marcus was born in Germany and grew up traveling the world, experiencing an array of cultures in the Philippines, Italy, and Germany—to name a few. His global experience and work in multiple languages have helped in building E&J Gallo and Sons' wine business in Europe. As a result of his efforts and those of his team, the Gallo brand is the largest in the German market. Frank ran E&J Gallo's Northwest region and is now the managing director responsible for E&J Gallo's sales and training on a global basis.

PREFACE

I often compliment my wife after she serves a delicious meal. Her quip in response is always, "It's all about a good recipe." If I could give you a recipe for finding and hiring great employees would you be interested? A good recipe relies on the specific ingredients, so too with the qualities of a great employee. There are certain qualities that we consistently find in successful employees and Hire on a WHIM is my system to help you find and hire those ingredients

Whether it's a multinational, multi-billion-dollar company or a small church; employees matter. And whether you are hiring out of high school, higher education or for the C-suite the qualities that make for great employees are the same.

When Hire on a WHIM was first released in 2010, I had no expectations as to whom or how many people it would reach. But I hoped it would become a resource to a few individuals and organizations looking to gain a fresh, viable and effective perspective on the hiring process. Since the original printing, the book and its concepts have helped thousands of hiring managers, and entire organizations have adopted the concepts of WHIM as a foundation for their hiring process.

If you are a hiring manager or involved with the hiring process you know the joys and frustrations of finding great talent. There is a way to hiring great talent consistently and WHIM will help you do that. Whether hiring for the mail room or the boardroom the ingredients for successful employees are the same; you'll want to hire WHIM. After each chapter you will find practical ideas and suggestions, be sure the questions and concepts align with your organization's HR policies and procedures.

There are two other groups of readers who have found WHIM helpful and this group has been a surprise to me. The first in this group are those preparing for an interview. I've been told, it's not too often you get to look at the other team's playbook, and indeed that is how this group has used WHIM. The second group is comprised of teachers, parents, mentors, and coaches who have realized that these principles are essential to teach to our youth. They believe as I do, that the four qualities of WHIM are established early in life. These teachers have taken the basics of WHIM and applied it to their world. Their input (especially Sara Jarolik, my friend and teacher in Texas) has been essential in the book I'm currently working on, Character on a WHIM.

I decided to write the second edition to address questions and concepts I was faced with by so many experienced managers who attended a Hire on a WHIM seminar. These questions prompted two new chapters that looked at the importance of onboarding and how to maintain WHIM in our employees and in our organization's culture. The real payoff for every organization is that the better job organizations do with the above, the better the retention rates.

The beauty of WHIM is its simplicity. Once you learn WHIM you will never forget it and it will be the rubric that you will use to evaluate most people you interact with. The final benefit of WHIM also applies to all readers. When the reader finishes WHIM he will come to realize that these qualities not only make for great employees, but these qualities are the foundation for being a successful person regardless of age or role. May this book challenge us all, to become better versions of ourselves.

On a personal note, since the original creation and printing of WHIM, new opportunities have opened up for me, and the concepts described in WHIM have been validated through national and international media coverage. But the most satisfying experiences for me have been hearing from readers. You can find me on Facebook (Words of WHIMsdom) and Twitter (@whimuniversity), and via email. I value your input and feedback, not to mention your stories on the impact WHIM has made and continues to make on your lives and organizations.

This Second Edition includes two new chapters born out of just such conversations with readers. As a result, many people have asked if it is enough to just hire WHIM. The answer is no. Business leaders, managers, employees, and prospects must be intentional in the creation—and maintenance—of WHIM in their lives and their organization's culture. Without diligent and ongoing nurture and encouragement, even the greatest hires will slip in job performance, interest and dedication. Employers, employees, and job seekers alike must make every effort to understand, cultivate, and maintain these outstanding qualities.

Garrett Miller 2019

CHAPTER 1:
ANOTHER ONE BITES THE DUST

"I want to make a lot of money and not work too hard."
-Response from a recent graduate when asked about
goals during a personal interview

"You're resigning? Why?" Jack Woodward grimaced and felt his face turn flush.

"A couple of reasons," Jen Campbell said.

Jack sat back in his chair and took a long breath. The more he listened to Jen's reasons, the more upset he became. He liked some aspects of Jen's work and considered talking her out of quitting, but the effort didn't seem worth it. He'd probably end up just having the same talk a month down the road. He'd had it with the mindset of the recent crop of hires.

"HR will contact you about how to close out," he answered once Jen finished outlining her reasons.

After the call, he sat at his desk and ran his fingers through his hair in frustration. He thought of the time he invested in Jen and now he had to fill another open position. "You know what? I'm done hiring recent college grads. If they don't have five years of quality experience—forget it." They didn't know how to work, Jack thought. They aren't interested in digging in to learn what it takes to succeed in this industry, they're hard to train and want to be complimented on nearly every task. "D-O-N-E." In frustration, he threw his empty coffee cup toward the garbage can, which of course missed. That about sums it up. Thought Jack.

His frustration was justified. After all, Jen was the third employee to resign from his team in a year and a half. Two of the three departures were recent college graduates; the third was a lateral transfer from a competitor with limited experience. Jack looked at his second monitor and clicked on his file marked recruiting. He smirked as he surveyed the articles he had saved, each identifying the problems with hiring this younger generation. He called his manager to deliver the bad news. While he waited for her to pick up, he opened a few of the articles and quickly scanned each for a few statistics—just in case. He took a deep breath.

"Good morning Jack."

"Hi, Carol, I hope you had a great weekend." He paused as she responded. "I have an update on one of my employees. I just got a call from Jen Campbell—she's decided to pursue other opportunities." He heard silence on the other end. Jack grimaced again.

"Wow, sorry to hear that," Carol Chang answered. "Was this expected? Did she give any reasons for leaving?"

"Several, and we've heard them all before."

Without waiting for Carol's answer, Jack continued. "I've been researching the recent turnover on my team," he said, looking at his screen. "Jen seems representative of her generation. Listen to how this article describes what they are looking for in a job."

- "They want flexible hours and don't want to be judged by the time they put in but the work they get done."
- "They continually expect recognition and rewards."
- "They want more communication and one-on-one conversations with their bosses. Seem to me like they just want their hands held."
- "They have an excellent understanding of the work/life balance— on the life side."
- "They're hard to motivate and incentivize."
- "They tend toward an entitlement mentality."

Jack clicked another article. "This other survey even describes them as 'mature based on inexperience, which makes this group a real gamble.'"

Carol interrupted, "Jack, did this survey really concluded that this group is a gamble?"

"Well, those are my words, but they sum up what I read."

"If memory serves—"

Here it comes, Jack thought, but this time he would be ready with a rebuttal for Carol's usual line of reasoning.

"In the past eighteen months, you've had three direct reports leave your team." Carol paused. "Your turnover rate is about twenty percent higher than the rest of the team; hiring and training new employees is expensive. Then there's the cost of sourcing and interviewing, not to mention onboarding—"

"Sorry to interrupt, Carol, but all three employees Mike, Spence, and now Jen fit into this problem group these articles are referencing. They just weren't motivated to work up to their potential and when I held them accountable for tasks and assignments they folded. I don't think they have what it takes to make it in our organization."

He waited for a response, wondering whether Carol really understood his position. It was hard to explain what the day-to-day was like with employees who weren't motivated to do the work they were assigned, let alone have an eye toward the future.

"Listen, Jack, you've had a very successful career with this company. You've got great instincts and you know how to grow the business. But when you first took over the department you had a seasoned team. As people were promoted or moved on you've had a difficult time replacing and retaining talent."

Jack shook his head. Nervously drumming his fingers on his laptop, he stared out the window. He dreaded where the conversation was heading.

"Being successful in your last position doesn't automatically make you a well-rounded manager. Hiring and holding onto great talent are two of the hardest but most important tasks for a manager—and they're both skills you have to improve on."

"Carol, with all due respect, I know the type of people it takes to win— I'm a winner. The reason these last three employees didn't work out is that HR keeps sending me to college campuses and job fairs to recruit. They send me resumes that have been sourced by online services and though they look great on paper it's just not translating into the workplace. It's a total waste of time—and I think the exit numbers show that. From now on I only want to look at seasoned talent."

And that was the crux of it. He was tired of investing time and energy, not to mention budget, training people who wouldn't stick around. He heard a faint sigh on the other end and knew Carol wasn't done.

"Listen, Jack, I'm well aware of the recruiting and hiring data for this current generation; every employee segment has them. But, frankly, I think this group you've been referencing can bring a lot to the table. And I don't think the problem is just who you've hired. I think you may be missing something in how you're hiring—meaning the interviewing process."

Jack closed his eyes. He could tell there was more, and if he valued his job, he knew he'd better listen.

"I want to make a suggestion," Carol said. "I'd like you to call a colleague of mine, Davis Walker. He has worked for the organization for more than twenty years and has developed a great eye and ear for talent. He'll teach you his system of how to hire 'on a whim', as he puts it. I'll text you his contact information."

Feeling trapped, Jack glanced down at the incoming text, "All right, I'll reach out to him."

"Trust me, Jack. This will be a great investment—in your career, as well as the future of your department, not to mention the organization. Let's talk again after you and Davis connect."

Jack thanked Carol and hung up, but all he could do was stare at his laptop and the statistics that proved he was right. Not only did he have yet another opening in his department, but he now looked inept to Carol. On top of that, she wanted him to contact someone who had been with the company so long he was probably about as in touch as yesterday's news. Even worse, he'd have to actually listen to this guy and report back.

"I know what the problem is," Jack fumed. "I'm the one in the trenches."

Wanting to get the call to Walker over with, he tapped the phone number, added it to his contacts and then called Davis. The phone rang once and immediately went to voicemail. Jack left a message and secretly hoped Walker wouldn't call back. At least I called, he thought. Then he thought back to Carol's comment, that this Walker guy would teach him how to "hire on a whim."

Yeah, that's how he was going to run his department now, on a whim. With a smirk, he clicked the file closed and went on to more important matters.

About an hour later, his phone buzzed. He glanced over and saw Davis Walker's name, clenched his fists in frustration and answered.

"Hi, Jack, Davis Walker returning your call."

Jack winced. "Uh, thanks for calling." Carol Chang wanted us to touch base. She said you might have a few hiring tips for me."

"Yes. I just got off the phone with Carol. She speaks very highly of you and she's got great instincts. When can we meet?"

Jack paused. He was too busy for an in-person. "Thanks, but it's the end of month push and the office is pretty busy. How about a quick conference call instead? You can give me your top ten hiring tips and maybe send a list of best practices."

Davis laughed. "We're all busy, Jack, but Carol asked me to give you real help in the hiring process and I promised I would. How is next Wednesday at three? Do you like coffee?"

Jack sat forward and looked at the coffee cup next to the garbage can. "Where do you want to meet?"

He would humor Carol and Walker, he thought, as he entered the date into his already packed calendar, and then maybe Carol would settle down and he could move past this.

Ten minutes later he got an email from Walker with what looked like assignments attached. Walker also wanted him to come with a printout of potential candidates along with their resumes and be prepared to discuss recruiting and hiring philosophies.

"Great," Jack muttered. "Now I've got homework."

Getting Started: A Self-Assessment for Those Seeking to Hire

1. Most people who hire view it as both opportunity and chore, usually more the latter. How do you view hiring employee talent? Do you see it as one of the most important aspects of your job or more as a necessary evil? What are the reasons for your perspective? What past experiences and/or current practices inform your opinion?

2. What are some of your personal philosophies on recruiting and hiring talent? What overarching themes drive your hiring decisions? Can you list them? Are they consistent from one hiring decision to the next?

3. Do you know others in your organization who consistently hire great talent? Ask to sit in on a few of their interviews, whether in person, by phone, or via video call. Take note of the questions they ask and the way in which they approach hiring. What drives their hiring decisions and why? Make it a goal to sit in on at least one interview per quarter.

4. Have you hired college graduates or those with just a few years of experience? If not, is it due to negative realities and/or perceptions? What are the sources of these realities and/or perceptions?

5. Whether on instinct or by intention, do you avoid or gravitate toward certain groups—recent college graduates, lateral hires, salespeople, or athletes, for example? What are your perceptions of these groups and why do you hold these viewpoints?

6. How many people have left your department in the past year? Is your turnover rate consistently higher or lower than the organization's average?

7. What were their reasons for leaving? Reconsider what they said to you directly and/or in exit documentation; there are valuable lessons to be learned.

8. Think of the last five employees who have left your team. Write down the skills, traits, talents or aptitudes that were weak or missing, that eventually lead to a critical disconnect.

CHAPTER 2
LAYING THE FOUNDATION

"Time spent on hiring is time well spent."
-Robert Half

Jack sat in the café, still grappling with the third resignation in eighteen months and that his department director, Carol Chang, had prescribed remedial training for him, to bolster his hiring capabilities.

This is ridiculous, he thought. I don't need a hiring coach. All I've had are a few bad hires. He barely noticed the man approaching his table.

"Excuse me, are you Jack Woodward? I'm Davis Walker."

Jack stood and was greeted with a firm handshake. Davis stood a few inches taller than Jack and was casually but neatly dressed.

Jack indicated the chair opposite. "I'm sorry you got dragged into this, Davis. I guess Carol is a bit concerned."

"No worries, this will be fun." Davis set his laptop on the table. "Why don't we start with you sharing your take on why we're here."

Jack sighed. "Unfortunately, that's easy. I've had three bad hires in less than two years—each was a recent college graduate or a hire with just a few years' experience. Bottom line, they don't know what they want to do, or they think they do then change their minds. They're hard to coach and motivate. They also focus on the short-term and don't take an interest in learning more about the department, organization or market. It's clear to me that hiring candidates from this generation is a mistake."

Davis studied him briefly. "I think the problem is less about who you're hiring and more about what you're hiring. What I mean is that in my experience there are three qualities each candidate—regardless of what

19

category of employee we're talking about—must have before you hire them, regardless of when they graduated or how much experience they've had."

"Three qualities? Perfect, that's just what I need—an easy fix." Jack took out his tablet. "Okay, what's the first quality?"

Davis looked at Jack's tablet with a smile. "Glad I sparked your interest but let's not get ahead of ourselves. First, I'd like to hear how you sourced the three colleagues who left."

"HR used a variety of recruiting tools then prescreened all three candidates, not that it did much good. The way I see it, the departures have more to do with the type of candidates HR is sending me than my hiring capabilities."

"It's easy to blame HR, Jack," Davis said with a shrug. "But you ultimately hired them. By the time you and I finish working on this, you'll be hiring with confidence, regardless of where your candidates were sourced or who sourced them."

"I do hire with confidence," Jack protested. "I just seem to hire poor candidates confidently!"

Davis laughed. "When I started I was in exactly the same position. I went through a hiring class, had my list of questions, performed practice interviews—then came my first opening and my first opportunity to hire."

"Complete disaster?" Jack said excitedly.

"No, she was terrific, one of my best hires ever!"

Jack shook his head. "I wish I had that problem."

"No, ended up working against me because I thought I had this hiring thing all figured out. It took six years and a lot of costly mistakes before I asked for help. You have the benefit of working for Carol, who's passionate about hiring great talent. And you have the advantage of learning how to hire correctly earlier in your career."

"Maybe, but lately I've come to hate the process."

"That's why it's important to start at the beginning—with the first step in the hiring process—every great hire begins with sourcing. It sounds like you rely on HR for most of yours, right?"

"I also keep a running file." Jack opened a folder and pulled out four resumes. "Here are the hardcopies you wanted. These first two were sent from current employees in my department. This other is a family friend and this last I pulled off our HR website."

"That's a start. But when did you last speak with these candidates?"

"It's been a few months—I haven't had any openings, so I haven't been in touch."

Davis reached over and picked up the resumes. "You say these first two are from current employees? I'm sure the thousand-dollar finder's fee had nothing to do with these." He smiled. "Whenever I hear someone say something like, 'A good friend is looking to get into the industry,' or 'She's a good candidate,' followed by all the reasons I would like the person, I always ask, 'Is he or she better than you?'"

Jack sat up. "What do you mean, better than you?"

"Think about it. If I hire an employee referral and the candidate isn't better than my current employee, I'm bringing down my team's average, aren't I?"

"I guess that's true. I never really thought of it that way." Jack instinctively reached for his tablet and paused as he wrestled with his pride; maybe there was more for him to learn. He casually clicked on a new document and tapped out what would be the first of many tips.

Davis leaned forward. "If you really want the best team you can have, each person you hire has to be better than the last. When I say better, I mean that they are going to add value to your team, maybe by experience level, skills, talents, attitude or energy level it could be a myriad of things." Davis paused. "Does that make sense?"

"I think so. A baseball coach needs diversity so he wouldn't hire nine great third basemen. And it's not enough to hire capable players. He needs to hire better players, players that fill in gaps and who raise everyone's effectiveness." Jack smiled. "I should ask the guy who submitted these two whether they're better than he is."

Davis nodded. "Now you've got it. As you start asking your people that question and share your reasoning, you'll get fewer resumes. But the ones you get will be of a higher caliber."

Jack grabbed the two remaining sheets. "Don't even bother looking at these—I'm pretty sure if I asked that question, they wouldn't survive the test." He pauses for a moment. "And by asking that question, I'm forcing the one who is submitting the recommendation to place their reputation on the line and that will help eliminated low-value submissions. I love it."

Davis nodded and looked at Jack's now empty file. "This means you have an opening but no viable candidates. In a situation like this, with each day that goes by you feel more pressure to hire so your standards start to fall. The longer the position is open, the greater the pressure to hire and—"

"The more I'll be more prone to a hiring mistake."

"Exactly. So, the first step in great hiring is to always have a viable—and current—pool of candidates, people you contact regularly, and not to wait until there's a need before you reach out. Do you have a system set up for that? For starters, do you have a relationship with a local college and a headhunter or corporate recruiter?"

Jack shook his head. "My experience with recent grads hasn't been good and I don't see myself developing a relationship with a college anytime soon and HR usually does the busy work of sifting resumes." He waved his hand. "Besides, after the last few departures—I'm done with colleges."

"I understand your frustration but don't pass judgment just yet on recent grads. A good strategy is to have a multi-pronged approach. Definitely, engage with a corporate recruiter or an online service you trust but let me prove to you why colleges and universities are among the best places to find great talent." Davis finished his tea. "And since you don't have viable candidates for the position that just opened up why don't we try my system? I'll upload a few resumes for you to evaluate. I'll also send a PowerPoint I put together—Instincts and Insights. Instincts play a vital role in hiring but you must make sure they're filtered through insight. Insight is knowing why you feel the way you do."

Great, more homework. This wasn't quite the quick process he had envisioned. "Okay," he said, taking a few more notes. "But Carol mentioned something about hiring on a whim so all this shouldn't take long, right?"

Davis laughed. "Hiring on a whim is not about how to hire quickly. It's a working philosophy about what to look and listen for in a candidate to help you make the right choice—consistently. I wish I could wave a wand or say a few magic words that would make you a great hiring manager, but it takes a little more than one conversation over coffee. You need to trust me on this."

Jack started to sigh then caught himself. "Sounds like a long and painful process."

Davis shook his head. "Hiring the wrong candidate is the long and painful process. We'll learn how to avoid that. Carol has always said that hiring great talent is the most important job you do as a manager. I think you'd agree, right?"

Jack gave a reluctant nod.

"If you want to become better at hiring, I know I can improve your skills. But you have to invest in the process."

Jack smiled. "I guess I don't have much of a choice."

"Then let's meet next Tuesday, same time and place." Davis got up from the table. "We'll only take about fifteen minutes but call me if you have any questions."

"I will." Jack shook Davis's hand.

Jack drank the rest of his coffee as Davis headed for the door, Jack sat turning his cup. I really don't need this, he thought. It's a waste of time. But he needed a replacement for Jen and the sooner the better. That meant he had to start interviewing. He crushed his cup and pitched it in the garbage.

Outside the café, Davis got into his car and thought about the meeting. Jack wasn't the most excited pupil, but he hoped they made some headway.

"Let me make that call now," Davis muttered. He took out his cell and scrolled to Susque State College and tapped the phone number.

"Susque State, Diane Raines."

"Diane? Davis Walker."

"Davis, how are you?"

"Doing great. What's happening?"

"Busy, as usual, trying to get these seniors ready for prime time. What can I do for you?"

"I was wondering if you could help me set up an interview day in a couple of weeks. I have an opening."

"Hey, that's terrific. Send me a description. I'll post the position today and have the resumes forwarded automatically as they come in."

"You know I need your best, right?"

Diane laughed. "That's all we have here at SSC."

"In that case, I need the best of the best, and thanks, Diane. See you in a couple of weeks."

Davis drove out of the parking lot. He certainly enjoyed working with SSC, he thought as he headed to his next appointment. The first time he visited the campus for interviews was seven years ago. The first two years he hadn't hired a single graduate, but each time he returned he built stronger relationships with the Career Services office and the faculty. Davis was always quick to provide feedback and soon they knew the type of candidate he was looking for. Now they automatically funneled some of their best candidates his way.

"Best investment I ever made," he said.

Begin the Hiring Process

1. What are some of the best ways to source candidates:
    *   Start by mining your best current employees for referrals. Employee recommendations are great sources of reliable candidates.
    *   For recent grads: Career Services personnel, college professors, other faculty, sports coaches, and alumni who know you, are all great sources for a higher quality graduate interview.
    *   For the more experienced worker recommendations: Networking with coworkers, friends, family, and vendor relationships is a good way to mine sources for potential referrals.
    *   Always be recruiting. As a hiring manager, you should always be listening, watching and building your file of viable candidates. Pass out business cards to those who impress you or who seem like a good fit.

2. What important principles should you as the person doing the hiring consider when one of your best employees comes to you with a potential candidate?
    *   Always try to hire up—think about improving your team's average and skillsets with each new hire. What gaps or weaknesses does your current team have? Find out which skills and gifts these new people will bring to your team.
    *   Have those who are referring candidates ask themselves, "Is the person I'm referring better than I am?" You'll get fewer referrals, which will reduce the amount of time and energy you have to invest in reviewing them, but the referrals you get will be of a higher caliber.
    *   An added bonus of internal referrals is the employee often has a vested interest in the candidate's success and may play the role of mentor in order to assure the employee's reputation is preserved.

3. What are some concrete ways to get the most from your HR department?
    *   Develop stronger relationships with the employees in the department. Don't just call when you need something; keep in regular touch with them.
    *   Volunteer for job fairs and interviewing days. If they see your

commitment to help them meet their goals, they will respond in kind.

- Offer to help with reviewing and sourcing perspective candidates. You just might come across a few candidates you may want to pursue.
- Does your HR department reach out to colleges, placement services, or graduate programs? If so, offer to represent the company.
- Invest in your HR department, and they will invest in you.

4.   How do you get the most out of college and university recruiting?
Develop strong relationships with one or two colleges or universities, especially those well-known for majors that reflect your organization's sector.

- Spend time with people in the college or university Career Services office and treat them as if they are your customers. They can become your most reliable sources of quality candidates.
- Keep in mind that Career Services personnel want a long-term relationship with you and your company. If they believe you're committed to their institutions, they'll be committed to you. A few ways you can invest in a college:
  - o   Offer to give a talk on your industry, your career path, interviewing skills, resume, tips, developing an effective LinkedIn profile, working with recruiters or working with online application services.
  - o   Offer to be a mock interviewer for students looking to better their interviewing skills.
  - o   Allow Career Services to use you as a source for an informational interview.
  - o   When you don't have an opening, you may find value in participating in recruiting events anyway. This demonstrates your commitment to the college or university, and you can build relationships that may eventually turn into hires. Always begin the interview letting the candidate know that you don't currently have an opening, but you are always looking for great candidates. If you find a great candidate, ask if you could reach out every few months because you would like to stay in touch and if there is an opportunity, you'd like to restart the interviewing process.
  - o   Try to interview candidates at least once a quarter. This keeps you fresh and prepared for unexpected job openings.
- See the bonus chapter by Jim Thrasher, Director of Career Services

at one of the most successful Career Services offices.

5. How do you get the most out of job fairs?
    - Expect to meet a diverse group of candidates. So, keep an open mind. These venues are great places to interview a few individuals who don't precisely fit your current template.
    - Develop strong relationships with a few of the regular job fairs in your area. Attend them to keep abreast of trends and stay connected with other like-minded recruiters and headhunters.

6. Recruit while you work:
    - Some of the best talent is found in your workplace. Always be interviewing, even while at work.
    - Observe and take note of the colleagues with whom you work. This is a great way to evaluate their skill sets and gifts.
    - Mine your competition: Always be ready to introduce yourself and hand out a business card to talent you see in the marketplace. For example, ask a successful, hardworking competitor or vendor, if they are ever interested in learning more about your company, you'd love to buy them a cup of coffee. A casual conversation can serve as a screening interview.
    - Ask your trusted vendors who they might recommend if they were hiring.
    - Who provides your vendors with excellent customer service, and who do they enjoy working with?

CHAPTER 3
INSTINCTS AND INSIGHTS

"If we are to learn to improve the quality of the decisions we make, we need to accept the mysterious nature of our snap judgments".
                                                                    -Malcolm Gladwell

In route to his second meeting with Davis, Jack quickly changed lanes and headed toward the exit. He was anxious to get on with the interviewing process. "I'd rather be interviewing than listening to him retell war stories," Jack said as he headed down the off-ramp.

He had to admit, though, that the PowerPoint presentation was interesting, and there were some strong candidates in Davis's resumes. Jack pulled into the café parking lot, grabbed his tablet, and headed inside.

Davis was sitting toward the back. On the table sat a Grande cappuccino, he had ordered for Jack.

"Thanks for the coffee." Jack slid into the open seat. "Are you drinking the same?"

Davis smiled. "I don't drink the hard stuff anymore—just herbal tea."

Jack pulled out his tablet and resumes and looked at his watch. What were the odds this would only take fifteen minutes, he thought. "All right, what did you want to cover today?"

Davis took a sip of tea. "Did you get a chance to look over the presentation?"

"Yes. Over the weekend." Jack touched the tablet screen and launched the presentation. "It was—interesting."

"Why do you think I had you review it before we start interviewing?" Davis asked.

Jack looked at him. "Well, I was always told to go with my gut, so I'd say your point is that instincts play a big role in hiring the right talent."

Davis nodded. "Right. And?"

"Even though I might have limited interview time with a candidate I can quickly make accurate decisions based on my experience, knowing what good and bad employees look like. We've all seen superstars and falling stars, right?" Jack tried to read Davis's expression.

Davis gave a nod. "Sounds like you took away some good points. But to make good, quick decisions you need more than experience. The main takeaway from the presentation is to know your prejudices—that's where insight comes into play. If you're not careful, unfiltered instincts, like prejudices, can lead you down a wrong path."

Jack shrugged. He thought he kept a pretty open mind during an interview. "I agree with what you are saying. I'm pretty good at keeping any prejudices I may have in check."

May I challenge you, Jack? How do you feel about the crop of candidates who have been graduating these past years?"

Jacked began to speak and stopped. He took a breath to speak again and then sighed. "Ok, busted. Isn't that different? I mean, I have evidence of their shortcomings."

Davis slid his cup aside and shook his head in disagreement. "It is a great example. We all have our reasons for our opinions, but we don't see our biases until later, sometimes we need others to point them out. I always thought I had good instincts and could read people well—until Steve." He shook his head again. "In reality, the downhill slide started with Anne, an employee who had been with the company for six years and on my team for three. She was nice but lacked motivation. She did just enough work to get by and had trouble with time management and with organizing her personal schedule. The same problems spilled over into the job. She also lacked a strong work ethic, which made her unproductive, so other employees had to pick up the slack."

Davis leaned forward. "When Anne left, I felt like I needed to recoup the years she cost the company. Instinctively I began to look for Anne's opposite, someone with a strong work ethic, so I set out to find that specific quality. I went to a hiring conference and interviewed five candidates. Some had good backgrounds but lacked the fire I was looking for. Then in walked Steve, a former Special Forces soldier who had just left the military. My prayers were answered!"

Jack nodded. "Perfect, I'll bet he has a great work ethic."

"That's what I thought. During the interview, Steve started telling me about all the hard training and fieldwork he did. As he talked, I pictured him sleeping in the desert, carrying fallen comrades to safety and participating in covert operations."

Jack smiled. "Sounds perfect."

"When he told me about the advanced training classes he attended, I knew he was the real deal, someone who wasn't afraid to work and was looking to be challenged—the perfect fit for my team and a great way to make up for lost time and energy."

Jack gave a nod. "I'd think the same."

"At first, he started out just as I expected—he was on fire. For example, I usually meet my reps at seven-thirty in the morning at a café in their area. Although I made a habit of getting there early, Steve would always be earlier."

"Sounds like a dream come true."

"It looked that way. So, we'd grab a hot drink and then be off and running. We visited Steve's bigger accounts and he knew everyone. We hit all the departments and he introduced me to key people. It was a full day of seeing customers, seven or eight to start. By the end of the day, I was exhausted. Every day with him was like that—a day at boot camp."

Jack sensed a caveat coming. "That's great! You must have been proud to have picked a winner."

Davis smiled. "It gets better. After the first few meetings, I got to the café even earlier. Again, Steve was already there. He saw everything as a competition, including beating me to coffee—or tea. In short order, our days got even more intense. We went from seeing seven or eight customers a day to twelve to fifteen a day."

"Man, that's crazy." Amazed, Jack shook his head. "Most reps have a hard-enough time seeing eight. I'd love to have a Steve on my team."

"Tell me about it. One day, Steve saw twenty customers. Twenty!"

"That's incredible." Jack was smiling, but Davis wasn't. "I don't understand. You got the person you wanted, with the qualities you were looking for. Your instincts led you to the right hire. Sounds like you're not disproving your point but confirming it."

"I didn't hire someone with the qualities the job required. I hired someone with the one quality I was looking for."

"But that was important, wasn't it?"

"It was but even though Steve was an incredible worker and competitive, he lacked certain qualities Anne had—."

"—Like the ability to show up late and leave early?"

"Ha. There's certainly some truth there but more like kindness, humility and the ability to get along with others. Not to mention the ability to understand that there's more than one way to solve a problem. Anne might have lacked organizational skills, but Steve thought he had the job figured out and he was going to do it his way, regardless of any feedback his colleagues, customers, or I provided. And he saw everything else the same way. There was no latitude in his approach to work."

Jack sat for a moment processing what he heard. "So, you went from being frustrated with Anne who didn't work much to being frustrated with Steve who worked—well—like a bull in a china shop."

"Exactly! With the internal hiring grid I set for myself, I let the pendulum swing in the opposite direction and it stayed there. Eventually, Steve's behavior wreaked havoc across the board. He alienated himself from his team, his peers, even his customers—unfortunately, he took the same one-sided approach with them. To try and 'fix things', I spent a lot of time with him. First, I tried mending fences with those he left in his wake, making excuses for him and trying to defend his actions. Then I tried to set parameters, which he resented. And he wanted to get promoted quickly. I finally had to tell him that if he didn't change, he'd never get promoted."

Jack winced. "Talk about a difficult coaching session!"

"Definitely. Long story short—I failed Steve and the company because I hired him based mostly on instinct and not much on insight. By hiring to fill one basic need, I lost sight of what was best for the company, Steve and our customers. In the end, I had to let him go."

Jack nodded sympathetically. "I'm sure that happens a lot. I could easily see myself running through that exact same scenario."

Davis pointed to Jack's tablet, "That's what this is for. A lot of your initial instincts are good because they're based on experience. But you must be aware of your internal filters and grids, plus the baggage you bring to the decision-making process. I had my own ideas because I was determined to choose the opposite of Anne. So when Steve walked in it was disaster at first sight, though I didn't know it at the time."

Jack slid his tablet closer and tapped out a few more notes.

"There were other ripple effects, too, from my instinctive choice. For one, I made a wrong decision that was painful to both Steve and me. And there were hidden costs—like the time and effort to try to bring Steve in-line, the hours of coaching, and that he was in a job that wasn't right for him. It was an expensive lesson, but I learned a lot. The first thing I realized is that are some qualities I can teach and mold in my employees and some I can't. The qualities that can't be taught but are essential to every job are the ones we'll focus on in the next few weeks."

Jack's eyes grew wide. "A few weeks? I thought—no disrespect but my schedule is jammed—I'm not sure if I—."

"Easy Jack. You have to go through the hiring process to replace Jen. Right? I'm joining you through the process so that you have a better hiring experience. Besides, hiring correctly is going to save you more time than you could even imagine. We need to get this process right—the first time." Davis noticed Jack's posture was rigid. "Trust me, Jack. This system works!"

Jack leaned back in his seat and sighed. "I have to admit," Jack glanced at his notes and pointed to his last entry. "You've made some good points and challenged me. I know I have biases and I'm sure they're not helping me in my hiring decisions.

"Exactly the point. When it comes to your motives, you must be vigilant from the get-go. So, let's look at the resumes I sent. Go through and separate them based only on instinct. Put a Y for 'yes' on the top left corner of those we should see. Don't spend more than thirty seconds on each. Then go through again, spend a few minutes on each and ask yourself why you initially said yes or no and the filters that affected your decision. After you go through a second time, put a Y in the right corner of those you still think we should see."

Jack took the resumes. "Okay, but can you give me an example of a factor I might see on a resume that could affect my decision, where my instincts might lead me astray?"

"Great question. So, remember what we're talking about—instincts and insights. Take, for example, a student you might not interview because she attended a community college instead of a state school or well-known university. You might instinctively choose a person because he went to an Ivy League school. You might also pass over someone with a 2.9 GPA but accept someone with a 3.6 because you're sure GPA is tied to success. You might also reject a person who took longer than expected to complete a degree. You get the idea?"

Jack nodded. "I'll give it a shot, see if I can keep these principles in mind."

"Once you're done, draw a five-year timeline for each candidate based on their resume so you can clearly see their experiences and activity. Since these candidates are all recent grads, begin the timeline at the beginning of their senior year in high school or freshman year in college. Include everything on their resume and then look for gaps and inconsistencies."

Jack groaned. "That sounds an awful lot like homework."

Davis smiled. "Consider it groundwork. I'm always curious about a candidate's activity level. A timeline is a powerful tool to help you gain insight into your candidate's work ethic and activity. Oh, and for these candidates, remember to include clubs, sports, summer jobs, and part-time jobs. Listen to those resumes, Jack—they're trying to tell you something. Let's meet again next Thursday around three."

Instincts and Insights are important tools in the hiring process:

1. Hiring the best employee begins with knowing what you're looking for.
   - Know which skillsets and employee qualities your team currently needs and why?
   - Understand which non-negotiable qualities and skills you seek to hire for the position and why they are non-negotiable.
   - Are these traits and abilities documented and up to date?

2. Instincts and insights are valuable tools; balancing them is key.
   - Give credence to your instincts about candidates. Your instincts can be a great barometer because they are often built on experiences.
   - Your instincts must be balanced with insights into your internal filters. One way to gain insight is to make a list of what you feel are qualities that will make or break a candidate's viability. For example, take a candidate's GPA. If it is below a certain number will you not see him? Why? Do you have data that shows a correlation between success and GPAs over a certain threshold?
   - For each of your must-haves or won't-haves, make sure each stands the test of logic and reason. Have a trusted friend or coworker review your list and ask them to challenge it. Try starting with a blank list and have each of your must-haves fight to make the list.
   - Life events can shape our biases, be vigilant about understanding your preconceived notions and prejudices.
   - Once you select candidates to interview, go back and review the resumes to make sure your rules and litmus tests haven't eliminated worthy candidates.
   - Are your cutoffs, must-haves, and litmus tests based on facts, or are they untested guidelines or outdated rules of thumb?
   - If they're not based on facts, how might you make them more realistic?

3. A visual timeline is a powerful tool for gaining insights.
   - Create a visual timeline for every candidate, plotting work, school, and other activities over at least a five-year period. Note gaps for further inquiry. Include all activities in the timeline.

- The timeline for recent grads should start at the beginning of their senior year of high school.
- Timelines for more experienced candidates may need to be a few years longer than five years to get a feel for patterns and gaps.
- Note activities and jobs that overlap. These can give evidence of a strong work ethic and provide an opportunity to explore the prospect's ability to balance and organize a busy schedule.

Defining Terms:
- Instinct: All the time you've spent interviewing and working with rising and falling stars, in addition to your own interview experience as a prospective employee, has left indelible impressions to where can sense when someone is right or wrong. Your gut is an amazing barometer, and it's meant to influence your decision making. Therefore, don't leave your instincts out of the hiring process. But instincts don't work well when they're considered independently of other factors such as your insights.
- Insight: Is the discernment it takes to know why you feel the way you do about certain criteria, candidates and their qualities. Ask yourself if you have prejudices, fair or unfair, that needed to be challenged.

□

CHAPTER 4
'LISTENING' TO THE RESUME

"When someone shows you who they are, believe them
the first time."
-Maya Angelou

"Are you in the middle of a big trade Jack? How's the portfolio? Davis asked as he approached the café table with his cup of tea.

Jack looked up from his smartphone and smiled. "I'm cautiously optimistic, but mostly cautious." He put his phone aside and reached for and opened his folder. "In fact, some of these candidates look more promising than my portfolio. I have to say, there are a couple of sharp prospects here."

"For a bunch of untested candidates, you mean?" Davis pulled out a chair. "I've worked with Diane for years. She knows the type of candidates that I'm looking for; she makes my job a lot easier. So, you saw some potential?"

Jack handed over six "yes" resumes and four "no" resumes.

Davis picked up two and noticed an N on the upper left and then a Y on the right. "What made you instinctively say no to these, then change your mind?"

"For Denise, it was her major—childhood education struck me as a bad fit. But when I took a second look, I saw she had strong work experiences. I realized my initial gut reaction was to think of my third-grade teacher Ms. Swanson. Then I realized it wasn't fair to paint Denise in that box. Her work experience is impressive and diverse, so I feel she deserves a look."

Davis nodded. "Nice pickup—and the second?"

"Tom was a youth group leader at a faith-based camp, which didn't strike me as a good fit—just didn't feel right. I realized I shy away from things I don't fully understand"

"Why did you change your mind?"

"When I came across it the second time, I spent a few minutes trying to justify my initial decision. It then occurred to me that if he headed up a soccer camp, I would have been all over him. I understood that it was a prejudice not based on facts."

"Nice job." Davis gave another nod. "It takes strong insight, self-awareness and the willingness to examine your mindset to reach those conclusions." He looked through the "no" stack and stopped at the last candidate. "What didn't you like about this one?"

Jack looked at the resume. "Sarah had a 2.7 GPA and I just don't think that's good enough for my team."

Davis looked closer at the CV. "I agree that grades are important but when you look at her experience—" Davis turned the resume around and pointed to the work experience section. "It looks like she was busy discovering. I assume you created a timeline for her. What does it look like?"

Jack paused. "Her grades were too low, so I didn't do a timeline."

Davis took out a pen and clicked it. "Then let's work on it together. You read the dates and her different experiences. I'll fill in the timeline. Start with her senior year in high school."

Jack hesitated. He felt he had good reason not to do the timeline but looking over Sarah's work experience he now regretted that decision. "Aside from playing varsity softball for three years, she had her own catering business and ran that for two years. She was a student mentor and a Resident Assistant." Jack looked up a bit flushed with embarrassment.

Davis smiled. "Shall we continue?"

Jack grinned. "I can admit when I've made a mistake. I get it."

Davis took the pile of "yes" resumes, each now with a timeline attached, and stopped at the second. "What did you like about this candidate?"

"Mary had a 3.4 GPA in finance, that's a tough major. I thought she was worth seeing."

Davis scanned the attached timeline, which was nearly blank. "From experience, I can tell you I'd rather interview a candidate with a 2.7 GPA who worked several jobs, played sports, or was involved in extra-curricular activities than someone who did very little in all her years of college and still earned a 3.4."

Jack shook his head. "I know that finance can be a particularly difficult major and a 3.4 is impressive."

Davis set the resume and timeline on the table. "That may be true, but college is so much more than grades, especially these days, and so is the job you've got open. When I look at a resume, I want to see someone who has been active, responsible and involved—and in more than one area. The person you hire for the open job will need those same skills."

"Yes, I know, it shows a strong work ethic, right?"

Davis sipped his tea. "It doesn't just show a strong work ethic. It shows someone who's been busy discovering her calling."

Jack looked confused. "I'm not sure I follow."

"Students who are involved and active are in a discovery mode—finding out their likes, dislikes, strengths and, weaknesses. I've found that those who were active and diverse in their experiences, whether they knew it or not, were busy discovering what they were good at what they liked and didn't like. The more active they were in the discovery process the easier it was for both of us to determine if this job was going to be a fit or not.

Jack looked over several of the resumes nodding with surprise at their activity level. "Ok. Being busy is a good thing." Jack tapped his tablet and added to his growing list of best practices."

"Let me clarify something. Every candidate you interview will say that they are busy. The question is, are they busy with a purpose? Candidates who have been busy with a purpose tend to be more self-aware of their gifts and talents and logically seek out employment that will be a good fit for them. Does that make sense?"

"It does now," Jack said. He added, 'busy with a purpose' and then continued to define what that meant. "I like it. I'll look for candidates who have been busy with a purpose I gain some insight into their work ethic and I'm more likely to see clues as to where their interests and gifts lie."

Davis set the resume down. "People usually figure out their calling in two ways. The first and best way is by doing the hard work of discovering it during their years at college—and it's usually not found in a classroom or textbook. The second way to discover one's calling is after college—or on the job. Moving in and out of jobs, the trial and error method is painful for everyone."

Jack looked pensive. "That is a lot to discern in the few minutes I have in the interviewing process. Clearly, I've not excelled here. I agree—it's costly. I've got the scars from candidates who were poor fits to prove it."

"When both parties are doing their part, everybody wins. A candidate who has been busy in the discovery process will stand out because it will show up on her resume and in her answers during the interview."

"I can see now why this timeline and carefully looking over the resume and or application is so important. I need to look for candidates who have been busy with a purpose."

"Jack, let me share a great success story. I remember interviewing a young man who had an incredible resume, was busy with a purpose and who had a great interview."

"Let me guess, you hired him and he's now vice president."

"No, it was a successful interview because I didn't hire him."

"Maybe you and I define success differently."

"Stick with me, Jack. His activity level was amazing. Mission trips to Africa and to Chile. He worked a summer during college with an Indian tribe in Arizona, he volunteered at the hospital and he had a 3.6 as a pre-med student. As the interview progressed, I could see and hear that his passion was for medicine, children and for the poor. I began to probe his experiences and he lit up and became more animated. Everything in this encounter pointed him in another direction. I stopped the interview short and said, "Andy, I'm not going to hire you because to do so would be a disservice to the company, you and society. Everything about you screams of service, caring, and healthcare. In my opinion, that is where you belong."

"Ouch, you really said that? How did he respond?"

"Jack, I don't normally offer career advice during an interview, but this was clear. He had done a great job discovering his passions, gifts, and talents and they were not going to align with our job description. After some back and forth he agreed with me. Though there were areas that might align, in the long run, it would not have been a fit. It was successful because by uncovering and probing his gifts, passions, and talents we were able to avoid a mismatch."

"And you avoided a hiring mistake that I might make," Davis added to his notes and quickly summarized Jack's example. "I gotta admit, I've always placed most of my energies on the interview. I now see that time invested in the resume, application, and timeline make my interview much more valuable."

"Invest time reviewing the resume, application and the timeline for clues on a candidate's strengths and interests and your interview will be much more productive."

Jack smiled and looked back at Mary's resume again. "I thought she deserved an interview. But I guess that's why you call it 'listening' to the resume. The more varied and relevant the candidate's experience—in school, work, and life—the better and she just doesn't have enough."

Jack sat for a moment. "I wonder if that's what's been happening with my hires. They had the ability to do the job. And they each did well in the training so competency wasn't the issue. They just didn't like the job. Ultimately, it wasn't a fit for them." He looked at the resume. "I never thought of a resume this way." He shook his empty coffee cup. "Looks like I need a refill."

Prepare for the Interview

1. What are the benefits of candidates who have been "busy with a purpose"?
   - Their experience has given them greater insights into their strengths and weaknesses, and their likes and dislikes.
   - Active and experienced candidates have a better idea of their calling and are often better prepared to enter the workforce because they tend to seek out opportunities that are a fit for them.
   - Not all activities are created equal. Some, like being a resident assistant, may provide a greater opportunity for discovery than being a ticket collector.
   - Ask why candidates chose the activities they did. What did they learn about themselves? What did they like and dislike about each experience? What surprised them about the experience? Would they do it again? Why or why not?

2. When reviewing a candidate's resume, create and use a timeline; it will be a valuable roadmap that will shape the interview.
   - Using a timeline makes it easier to see whether a candidate was working two jobs at once or no job for a few months.
   - The timeline makes it easy to see when experiences stopped and started and easy to see where there were gaps in a candidate's history. There may be good reasons for the gaps, but at least with a timeline, you'll know enough to ask.
   - When using a timeline, look for patterns. Toward what skillsets, work settings, and job structures did the prospect gravitate and why? How long did the prospect remain in each position? The answers and patterns may provide insights into what they enjoy.
   - When there is overlap on the timeline indicating multiple experiences and or jobs at the same time, ask how they were able to manage and balance the demanding workload and did they do it successfully?
   - Use the timeline in advance of the initial interview to plot out each experience and activity the candidate lists on his or her resume or application. This will be an excellent resource during the initial interview as candidates walk you through their career and through any gaps and missing pieces.

3. When first reviewing a resume, how should you weight factors like

GPA, for example, as of high, medium or low importance, in determining which applicants to bring in for an interview?

- Using GPA as a measure of a candidate's fitness for a position should be a "soft" litmus test. Balance this achievement with the candidate's activities and experiences.
- In their proper context, grades make a difference when the subject matter or major is a key part of the position for which you're hiring. Grades also matter because they often reflect the prospect's commitment and ability to learn.
- If the individual's activity level is high, you can give less weight to the GPA. If there's no or low activity outside the classroom, expect higher grades.

4. What should you do if a candidate's GPA is less than your "cut-off"?
   - If you are concerned about a candidate's grades or ability to learn, then closely review the candidate's transcripts. One bad semester early on can significantly affect a student's final GPA. Many students begin their college careers with a rocky start then make significant improvements once they acclimate to an academic environment.
     - o My first semester ended with a paltry 2.1 GPA. I had to average a 3.15 GPA for each of the next seven semesters to pull my overall GPA up over a 3.0.
   - When reviewing a prospect's transcripts, look for solid GPA growth and positive trends. This may be an indicator of the student maturing throughout the semesters. To prompt discussion during the interview and to learn more about the prospect, ask what he has learned about himself or what changes she had to make in order to achieve her upward trend.
   - Ask the prospect if he had a GPA goal when he started classes. Was he able to achieve that goal? If so, why? If not, why not? What did he learn about goal setting and about himself through the process?

Defining Terms:
- Calling: The occupation that maximizes an individual's natural gifts, aptitudes, and talents. Employees will be more content and productive when there is a cultural and talent fit.
  - o A candidate will discover their calling, the question is: do you want them to do so before or after you hire them? Look for candidates who have done the hard work of discovery before you hire them.

*For more about calling, read *Hired 'Right' Out of College – From Classes to Career* (Garrett Miller, Dog Ear Press 2012).

CHAPTER 5
DISCOVERING THE FIRST QUALITY

"Talent is cheaper than table salt. What separates the talented
individual from the successful one is a lot of hard work."
-Stephen King.

Jack came back to the table with a fresh cup of coffee. "I thought you were going to teach me how to hire on a whim. This process seems like it's taking a lot longer than a whim," he joked.

Davis smiled. "Patience. There are no shortcuts when it comes to finding the best talent, patience."

Jack pulled out his chair. "Well, it's not like I'm going anywhere." Not without finding someone to fill the position on his team, he thought. And this time he couldn't afford to hire the wrong person.

Davis closed his notepad. "First, the qualities we're looking for are a combination of nature and nurture. And by the time we see our candidates, those traits are pretty well-established."

Jack moved his coffee aside. "Wait, are you saying that if candidates don't already have these qualities—and it sounds like you've got specific traits in mind—before I hire them, they'll never develop them?"

"What I'm saying is that the best candidates have already cultivated these qualities. I can't teach them, and neither can you. Nobody can. Candidates who don't possess them by now might learn them eventually. But we can't depend on 'eventually'. We need to hire people who already have the traits we need."

"Okay, I'll bite. Tell me what you look for."

"The first quality I look for is a strong work ethic. Everyone has a work ethic of some sort, but I look for someone with resilience, and grit, what used to be called stick-to-it-ive-ness."

Jack nodded and added to his notes. "Okay, a strong work ethic. What metric do I want to see on a resume that measures work ethic?"

Davis smiled. "We've already been using it. You can get a good grasp of a candidate's work ethic by checking the timeline. By using this tool, you can literally see how active and involved the person was in high school, college and after."

"Right, but I've been thinking—don't certain factors like course load in high school and college keep people from getting more involved?"

"In some cases, yes. But people who've developed a strong work ethic manage to stay involved in outside activities. The key word there is 'manage.' One element of a sound approach to work is the ability to manage your time." Davis pointed to Jack's stack of papers. "Here, pick one of the timelines and let's go over it."

Jack pulled out a timeline and set it next to its corresponding resume. "At first, this exercise seemed futile. But when I look at this timeline, I can see when the candidate's activities begin and end and where they overlap." He pointed to the work experience section. "For example, when I first looked at this position, I was impressed by the title that went with it and missed that the candidate only held the job for five months. But when I put it side by side with her timeline, the short time she spent in that role stood out. And it's not the kind of position a person would just up and leave. So, I'm going to ask her about that."

"Exactly," Davis agreed. "The timeline is a great tool because it creates a roadmap, showing each of the candidate's positions and how long he or she stayed with it. The timeline also triggers helpful questions like the one you just discovered." Davis took the stack of resumes and slid one of the initial "no" prospects across the table. "I can see why you passed on this one at first. Just looking at the resume, all you see is that she didn't work a job at all during the school year." He pointed to the activities section. "But she was on the volleyball team the first two years of college, held an elected position in her sorority, served as a big sister in her hometown, worked on the homecoming committee her last two years, and earned a minor in economics."

Jack looked at the resume. "Right. I had trouble getting past her minimal work experience and really didn't notice her outside efforts." He smiled. "My guess is you'll tell me she's been busy with a purpose and that all these different experiences helped her understand herself, what she's good at, what she likes doing, and what she doesn't enjoy or do well."

"Right," Davis agreed. "When I use the term 'work ethic', I'm not just talking about a paid job. I'm talking about a person's willingness, ability and commitment to be involved, especially if the activity is one the individual chose. You've done volunteer work, so you know that some of those roles are more demanding than paid jobs."

"That's for sure." Jack glanced at a few of the other timelines to see if he also captured the outside activities.

"High school and college are such formative times," he continued. "I guess if a candidate doesn't have a strong work ethic by the time we see them, then, he probably won't develop one anytime soon." He made a note. "But let me ask you this. Twice I've had to put an employee on a performance improvement plan because their work was not up to expectations. After a lot of additional paperwork, check-ins, ride-alongs and HR visits each employee eventually boosted their productivity. It seemed to work out."

Davis smiled. "You may not realize it but you're proving my point. There are two issues with performance improvement, especially when it's used to remediate qualities the employee should have had to start with. First, you can change work habits in the short term, often through micromanagement and pressure. But once you stop overseeing the employee what usually happens?"

Jack sighed. "Right, I see. They eventually fall back to their prior behavior—and performance."

"Correct. Now you've put in more time and effort, beyond onboarding and training, with little to no yield. Second and worse yet, you won't change how a person views work. People either embrace it because they're good at what they do and enjoy it and give you their best, or they don't."

Jack started to make another note and paused. "Isn't there an interview question I can ask to draw out the work ethic quality?"

Davis nodded. "One of my favorites is to ask what percentage of a candidate's education she paid for, including scholarships. I include scholarships because they don't just give those out—you must earn them. If a candidate has contributed significantly to her education—let's say twenty-five percent or more—I'm impressed. If a candidate has contributed little or nothing, I don't hold it against him. But he needs to show me his mindset on work in other ways."

"I like that question," Jack added that to his notes. "How else do you uncover work ethic?"

"I try to talk them out of the job."

Jack looked up. "What?"

Davis nodded. "That's right—I paint a worst-case scenario for the position. I talk about driving to a client's office in the middle of nowhere in the pouring rain, getting out of the car and stepping into a puddle, opening the trunk with one hand while holding the umbrella in the other to keep from getting drenched."

Jack grinned. "Sounds familiar."

"It gets worse. After slogging through the parking lot, you squeak across the lobby in soaked shoes only to hear the administrative assistant say, 'I tried your cell but it must have been off. We have to reschedule.' With every ounce of self-discipline, you regain your composure and with a tight smile, answer, 'I understand.' Then you head back through the lobby, force yourself back into the downpour, get back in your car and tell yourself you worked way too hard in life to be doing this."

Jack winced. "I've felt that pain."

"That's the point," Davis said with a nod. "Once I've set the scene, I look at the candidate and ask: 'Is this what you really want to do?' My point is to paint a bleak enough picture so that only someone with a strong enough mindset toward the position and a real desire for the job would say, 'I've been through worse. I know there will be bad days at this job, but I'll need to get through those bad days to get to enjoy the good days.'" Davis sipped his tea. "That, my friend, is the kind of heart you're looking for."

"I like that approach," Jack agreed. "And I certainly have some real-life examples to use. But you know as well as I do that some candidates will say yes no matter what you describe."

"That's where we as interviewers have to be engaged throughout the process. When I tell the story, I study the candidate, look for reactions, positive and negative. Then I probe a bit. I ask for feedback on the story. If I hear, 'Oh, I've done work like that before,' I investigate those experiences." Davis glanced at his watch. "Speaking of interviews, I'm doing one this afternoon." He took the last sip of his tea and began gathering his belongings.

Jack nodded. "I guess if the timeline looks great and we can't talk the prospect out of the job, we know he's not afraid to roll up his sleeves." He slipped his tablet back in its pouch. "But what about how they perform?" He got up from the table.

"At that point, if you're still interested, revisit the timeline and choose a few experiences or jobs and ask about projects or assignments they completed. What was the specific feedback he received and how did this compare to others he worked with? Listen for situations where he went beyond the call or worked late and ask what that entailed. Ask him to describe an occasion when he was most proud or discouraged during these experiences. The details of stories like those offer greater insights into the candidate's view of work so be sure to ask follow-up questions for example why he reacted or felt that way. Probing a bit deeper will also lead to areas that candidates may not be prepared for and I find those conversations to be the most revealing." Davis pushed his chair back. "I'm parked in front."

"So am I." Jack grabbed the two empty cups and disposed of them while he followed Davis to the parking lot. "I like asking questions a candidate is not ready for, they seem to produce more honest, transparent answers. But what about the term you used—calling?"

Davis nodded. "You mean vocation versus just a job. Well, when a candidate has been active, ask which activities she enjoyed most, what type of work she found most fulfilling and why." Davis stopped and excitedly turned to Jack. "That is another beauty of the timeline. As you work through each experience with the candidate you are listening for clues. What excites, frustrates, motivates and fulfills her. Pay attention to her answers because if her natural talents, gifts, and interests don't match your job description then there will be a disconnect. If she has been busy with a purpose, your decision to hire or not will be easier."

Jack made a few mental notes. "Got it. For example, if one of the aspects she enjoyed most in her last job was interacting with people, I need to probe a bit and see just how important it is to her. If I know this job doesn't need or use that gift, then I need to proceed with caution. One of my last hires was a capable guy but he never engaged enough with the position to give it a hundred percent, or eighty for that matter. I'm guessing I missed a few clues along the way."

"That's where his sense of vocation and fit—" Davis held up his key fob. "Is key."

"That's terrible. Hey, while we're on the subject, would you mind giving me the other two secrets?" A twinge of anxiety about filling his open position flashed on his mental to-do list.

Davis grinned. "Those will have to wait until next week when we meet at Susque State College. We've got six good candidates to interview, three recommended by people I respect." Davis opened the car door. "Hey, thanks for being prepared today. It allowed for a great discussion. Call me if you need me. If not, I'll see you next week."

Jack walked to his car and checked his watch. Thirty-five minutes. He smiled. How quickly time had flown—and surprisingly, the meeting hadn't been painful.

Mining the Resume and Application:

1. Work Experience and involvement in voluntary and extracurricular activities may reveal a lot about a candidate's work ethic.
   - Keep in mind that formal work experience isn't an absolute necessity on a resume for a recent graduate, but involvement is.
   - If a candidate didn't work at a formal job much or at all during high school and/or college, check to see if she was volunteering in meaningful organizations and/or actively involved in relevant groups or clubs. Follow up on these to make sure the experience is accurately noted in the resume.
   - For more experienced candidates, check to see whether there is a pattern in the work experience, for example, changing jobs or industries every two years. If the timeframes are shorter, probe the circumstances around the abbreviated stays.

2. Here are examples of what you should look for when assessing the activities in which a candidate was involved:
   - Look for activities that require commitment and dedication, for example, varsity sports and semester-long activities, such as choir, the debate team, internships, and drama club.
   - Prospects who put in more effort and show dedication as volunteers often carry those qualities over as employees.
   - During the interview, when you probe regarding work and/or non-work experience, watch for emotion, positive or negative, as candidates describe their involvement. Do they get excited talking about their successes, projects, overcoming obstacles? Do they seem emotionally disengaged from the interview and their experiences?
   - Ask specific questions about the candidate's involvement and how many hours were spent each week or month on each activity. Sometimes what looks like a time-intensive activity was more of a resume filler.
   - What did they learn from each experience, did it expose them to new challenges and opportunities? Note what these were.
   - Did they ask for more responsibility?
   - What challenges did they face and have to overcome to succeed?

3. Here are examples of questions to ask during the first interview:

- Ask the candidate for examples of jobs, classes, or activities that were stressful or difficult. Ask the candidate what he did and how he felt in those situations.
- What did she like most and least, and what did she find most and least rewarding about each job or position, and why?
- Ask the applicant to describe her most satisfying work experience and her worst experience, and to explain the "why" of each.
    - o Listen carefully to the answers to discern what aspects of the experience motivated the applicant.

4. Here are some key benefits to hiring an employee with work ethic.
   - They are more likely to follow through and complete a project on time and as requested.
   - They tend not to spend their time counting the hours, but instead put their heads down and work hard.
   - Their energy and enthusiasm are contagious.
   - They take pride in their work as it is a reflection of who they are.
   - There is less need to monitor their work which frees the manager up to invest her time elsewhere.
   - They are dependable.

Defining Terms:
   - Work Ethic: A set of values based on the moral virtues of hard work and diligence.
     - o Note: These values are acquired early and become part of one's DNA. A work ethic may be improved later in life, but it is non-negotiable and non-teachable. You must hire people who already possess this quality.
   - In short: A diligent response.

CHAPTER 6
WHAT A STRONG WORK ETHIC LOOKS LIKE

"Success usually comes to those who are too busy to be
looking for it."
-Henry David Thoreau

Davis and Jack traveled to Susque State College, where a full day of interviews awaited them. They walked into Career Services to meet with Davis's longtime contact, Office Manager Diane Raines.

"Good morning Diane." Davis smiled. "This is my colleague Jack Woodward. He's going to be joining me for the day and we're here to find him a superstar."

"Good to see you, Davis, and early as usual." Diane shook Jack's hand. "Nice to meet you, Jack. You came to the right place. I'm not one to brag but when it comes to talent—it's why ya'll keep coming back. Gentlemen follow me I'll show you where you'll be interviewing." She led them down the hall past a lounge to rooms set aside for recruiters.

"Thanks, Diane. Wow. You've done some updating since last time."

"Yes, we have." Said Diane proudly. "Our entire office has high-speed internet and each room has the latest audio and video equipment in case you need to conduct a video interview or if you need to have a colleague or interviewee join remotely."

Davis looked around as he set his tablet on the table. "I'm impressed. This is terrific."

"I'll be in my office if you need me." Diane left the interview room door open and went back to her desk.

"I'll conduct most of the interviews so you can observe and take notes. Then when we're near the end of an interview I'll turn to you so that you can ask a few questions.

Surprised and a bit annoyed at having to take a backseat during the process, Jack settled at the end of the table. He might not have the best system for sourcing candidates, but he knew how to interview.

Davis peered out into the hallway. "I see our eight o'clock is waiting, a good sign." He took out her resume and timeline. "Nothing bothers me more than a candidate who's late for an interview. If you're ready, I'll ask her in."

He went out into the hall, introduced himself to Sharon and brought her into the room where he introduced her to Jack.

"Hi, Mr. Woodward, nice to meet you." Sharon shook his hand and took out her tablet. "Hope you don't mind if I use this to take notes." She also set a hardcopy of her resume on the table, along with a hardcopy of the job description and the application she had downloaded and filled out.

They were off to a good start, Jack thought.

Davis settled in and looked over the papers in front of him and then smiled. "Sharon, I want this to be very conversational. I want to get to know you, so I'm going to set up a scenario to begin our discussion. Sharon let's say you and I went to high school together. I left after junior year, and here we are seeing each other after all those years. I'll ask you how you're doing and what you've been up to? Take me through your senior year up to today."

Jack quietly tapped his tablet and made a note.

Sharon thought quietly for a moment and then smiled. "For starters, my last year of high school was quite a year. It seemed like it hardly started when it was over. I played two varsity sports, fall soccer and spring lacrosse. And I was a member of the Entrepreneur's Club, where I served as the secretary. I also--."

"Tell me about your experience as the secretary and why that position?"

"Funny you ask. I didn't run for office is was more like an appointment. Sharon smiled. "I'm very organized. I like things in order and for things to run smoothly. The sitting president knew that about me and asked if I'd please take the position. I was glad to, it was an easy fit."

"It's nice when others recognize your gifts. And let's face it, as the secretary you have control of the agenda. So, who was really in charge?" Davis smiled. "If your meeting notes are public would you mind sending me a copy? I'd love to see an example."

"I'd be glad to. And shall I copy Mr. Woodward as well?" Sharon looked down and tapped out a note.

"Please do." Said Davis. "It sounds like a busy year. What else rounded out your senior year and what did the summer look like?"

"I played piano in the school's jazz band, that was a lot of fun. It was great." Sharon paused. "The summer after senior year I got a job as a bank teller and when I wasn't working, I'd go for runs, read, and spend time with friends."

"Bank teller? How did you get hired for that and how many hours a week did you work?" Davis interjected.

"The president of the club I was in, his mom was the manager. Sharon smiled. "I guess I had a little inside help. On average, about forty to forty-five."

"There's no need to apologize for networking. That is a very important skill to develop. Were you evaluated at the end of your summer?"

Sharon slid several pieces of paper out from under her tablet and passed one over to Davis. "I'm sorry I don't have a copy for Mr. Woodward. I didn't know there would be two of you. I can include it when I send my meeting notes."

"This is terrific." Davis checked the clock on the wall, "I'll look this over tonight." Davis continued to scan Sharon's timeline. "Why so many hours at the bank with such a busy schedule?"

"I come from a fairly large family—two brothers and sisters. If I wanted to go to college, I needed to help pay my way."

Jack made a note and cleared his throat signaling to Davis for permission to ask a question. Davis nodded. "What percentage of your education would you say you paid for?"

Sharon thought for a minute. "Once I pay off my student loans, it'll be about half."

Impressive, thought Jack.

"Sounds like a busy senior year followed by an even busier summer," Davis continued in the scenario as a recently reunited friend, "What did your college years look like?"

Sharon grinned. "Not much of a let-up there—I like to be busy."

She described her years in college as equally active as high school, playing four years on the varsity lacrosse team, playing intramural sports, and lots of student activities. When she finished, Davis sat quietly and studied his notes.

"What about the summer before your freshman year of college? It must have been hard with your friends going to the beach, staying out late and sleeping in—and there you were stuck working a forty-hour week."

"It would have been nice to spend more time with my friends." Sharon paused. "But the way I see it, every family's finances are different. I've always had to work for spending money and let's not forget gas, car insurance, my cell phone—those types of expenses. But after a long week, when I see money in the bank it gives me a sense of pride, not to mention stability. My mother always told me hard work pays off and she's right. I think I'm a better person for it. I have more appreciation for the things I've had to work for. But maybe that's just me."

"Great attitude," Davis affirmed. He scanned her timeline again. "I see you worked during college yet maintained a 3.3 GPA. Was that a difficult balancing act?"

Sharon laughed. "I can't say it was easy. My tendencies towards being organized and having routines helped a lot. Being a resident assistant was rewarding. I loved that job and I enjoyed my major. To be honest, being a student and an RA combined was still easier than working full-time at the bank, so I guess being busy is all relative."

Just as Sharon and Davis finished walking through her timeline, Jack's watch chimed signaling the end of the allotted time. He smiled. That was quick.

After answering Sharon's questions about Omega Industries, Davis handed her a packet entitled, "Your First Career Choice May Be Your Best."

"I'd like you to take a look at this. Omega has a terrific reputation for hiring and helping develop emerging talent into professionals and leaders. We invest heavily in training so that you have the tools to succeed." Davis watched as Sharon looked over the information. Then he stood to signal the end of the interview. "I hope we get a chance to talk again."

Taking the cue, Sharon did likewise. "I look forward to meeting with you both again." She nodded at Davis and Jack. "This has been a pleasure."

Once she left, Jack closed the door. "I can't believe how fast the time passed—I only got a chance to ask one question."

Davis grinned. "Yeah, I'm sorry I didn't leave more time for you. I also wished I had left enough time for her to ask questions. I have a feeling we'll be seeing her again."

"I hope so. That was great." Jack said excitedly.

"It's usually a good sign when an interview flies by. Did you notice how many questions I asked?"

"Not many," Jack said with some surprise. "Yet we still learned a lot about her." He looked at his notes. "You asked her a question about her senior year and interjected questions when you were looking for more information. It wasn't hard either. She was forthcoming and I liked listening to her story."

"That's because she enjoyed telling her story. It tells us something about how she views work. It also tells us what she enjoys doing. She has a good insight into her strengths, gifts, and aptitudes."

Jack paused. "But isn't that the goal of the interview—to see if the candidate has what it takes to be successful in our company?"

"Yes, we want to see that she has the right skills and interests to be a vocational fit but we are also trying to meet the real Sharon. Listen, every candidate we interview knows either specifically or generally what we are going to ask. We're going to hear the right answers. The second goal of the interview is to get to know the person. I don't want to meet a robot who can answer questions she already knows; I want to meet Sharon. If she is relaxed and speaks freely during the interview the more likely we are to see the real person. It's amazing what you'll learn, good and not so good once a candidate gets on a roll."

"So, you use the role-playing question with each interview?"

"I do." Davis pointed to his tablet. "Look at all the information that came from it. With an opening question like this, I can ask for details as she is telling her story. Questions like how she got a particular job, how many hours she worked, why she applied to certain colleges. The answers give you a sense of how she made those decisions, what makes her tick. And if you don't get to all your questions during the first interview, you have enough information to ask more specific questions later."

Jack nodded. "You certainly learn about a person's motivations."

"That and how candidates view themselves and their lives. Prospects with a clear self-image draw you into their story. When Sharon was telling hers, I got a sense of what she's passionate about because her tone and demeanor changed relative to the different experiences she was describing."

Davis closed Sharon's folder. "So how would you evaluate Sharon's work ethic?"

Jack laughed. "I don't need my notes for that one. If this college graduate was on my team, I'd say she would give one hundred percent, consistently."

Davis smiled. "This generation may have a different approach to work, but they bring amazing skillsets to the table. They're energetic and optimistic. And they understand social networking. New technology doesn't intimidate them. They're motivated by it. And they usually integrate it quickly, into both their lives and their jobs."

Jack looked pensive. "I think another advantage of hiring a recent grad is that I'd have a chance to create a strong working relationship. I still have that with Len, who first hired me. Even now I consider him a mentor and reach out on occasion when I need advice. I'd love to have that with my new hires. I guess I gave up on the prospect."

Davis shook his head. "Don't. You can still have that camaraderie. And when you hire the right qualities and the candidate uses his skills, they benefit the whole team. That enables you to cultivate the relationship and develop loyalty to both manager and colleagues. Those ties can reduce turnover and facilitate coaching because the employee sees you as her advocate."

"I hope so." Jack still didn't want to be too optimistic. "But I'd like to see a few more candidates like Sharon before I feel confident in my next hire. Because if I get it wrong again it'll be painful—for everyone."

Davis nodded. "I agree. That's why we're looking to hire traits that are both non-teachable and non-negotiable. When you hire someone with those qualities, you reduce the number of distressing situations like the one you're in now."

Jack put a check in the corner of Sharon's resume. "Let's see the next person on the list."

Discerning a Candidate's Work Ethic:

1. Here are some advantages of starting interviews with a strong, open-ended question like the one Davis used:

   - Asking a candidate to take you back five years and describe her professional journey takes her out of the expected question/answer format and into a more relaxed storytelling mindset. This scenario tends to draw the candidates out and may offer additional insight into her decision making, motivations, and passions.
   - The goal is to get to know the person, so get her talking.
   - Once the candidate is engaged in telling her story, you can gauge her motivation, intensity, and excitement by the way she speaks and how detailed she is in describing her involvement.
   - As the candidate walks through his story and timeline it will trigger questions, a desire for more detail, excitement and sometimes concern. Either take notes for a follow-up or don't be afraid to interrupt and have him address the question while he is telling his story. For example, as the candidate is talking about his movement from one department to another, you may ask any one, or several of the following:
     - Before you get to the new position. Tell me, what prompted the move?
     - How did you get the interview?
     - What did you like most/least about the position you were leaving?
     - How did you perform, be specific?
     - Did you get a recommendation from your former team lead?
     - How did you research the position you were moving into?
     - Was this a position you were hoping to settle in or were you looking beyond this to another department or position?
   - When candidates speak freely, they often provide information that may not come up in response to more structured and predictable questions. Being an active listener is essential in this process because there can be valuable clues in the small details.

2. Look for candidates who are busy with a purpose. It's easy to be busy without personal growth. Purposeful engagement with direction is entirely different:

- Candidates who are busy with a purpose are open to and looking for varied experiences and environments; these experiences help them grow and become well-rounded and help them gain insight into their strengths and weaknesses, likes and dislikes. You'd rather the prospect learn these insights on his time than yours.
- As you move through a candidate's timeline and story, look and listen for those whose choices of work and experiences are driven by a desire to invest in themselves and others. These mindsets translate well to the workplace as they push themselves and others to grow.

3. When the candidate talks about their college or work experience, do you get the sense that they were grueling years or did time fly by?
   - If you get a sense from the candidate that these years seemed to pass quickly, it's a signal that he was active and engaged, doing work he enjoyed, found fulfilling, and at which he is skilled.
   - If the prospect's time seemed to pass slowly, probe to see if there was a disconnect in fit. This may prove very valuable as you are evaluating a proper fit for your open position.
   - A candidate's experience can also feel arduous because of the manager, people, culture, industry, and environment she was working in. It could have simply been because it was a long commute. The important thing is to probe and look for insight as to how any of those scenarios might translate into your organization.

4. During the interview, if you learn of an experience the applicant didn't enjoy, you can still gain insights into his work ethic:
   - Ask how he handled the situation and was he still able to deliver good results.
   - Ask if the candidate sought or was prescribed coaching and how he responded to it? Was there a desire to learn and get better so that he could succeed in his areas of responsibility?
   - Ask what the candidate learned from the difficult experience.

5. When a candidate has a hard time discussing herself or has little excitement in telling her story, it should send up a red flag:
   - If the candidate can't be enthusiastic about her work or life experiences, there may be concern that she won't be able to be excited or motivated for your organization's goals. If you pick this up, probe what motivates her and gets her excited. As you walk through her timeline listen for motivation and excitement.

- An interview that drags on may indicate that something is missing. Once the interview is over, consider what may have made it seem so long. Did you feel you had to do most of the talking? Were there lots of uncomfortable moments of silence? Did it seem like you had to drag answers from the candidate? Were her answers short and unproductive? Did she seem closed off in her tone, body language, and demeanor? These are just a few examples of what can inhibit the flow of an interview.

- If an interview drags on be aware that you are not contributing to it because you are sleepy, frustrated, exhausted, biased, or disengaged. If you find yourself in any of these situations it would be better to stop the interview, ask to be excused for a few minutes and walk outside to clear your head and reorient yourself. You owe an interviewee your best. That is the strong work ethic that you must bring to the interview.

- An interview that flies by is usually a good sign. It may also mean that you are very excited about the candidate. If this is the case, be sure you are not allowing your excitement to gloss over gaps and red flags. What you look over now in haste and excitement may produce long-term regret. You've heard the term, term buyer's remorse, this is what I call, hire's remorse.

CHAPTER 7
IT MUST BE A FIT

"The question who ought to be boss is like asking who ought to be tenor in the quartet? Obviously, the one who can sing tenor."
-Henry Ford

Jack and Davis wrapped up their last interview of the morning at Susque State College with Kelly, a personable senior with a strong GPA who appeared to have a lot going for her. Her timeline reflected a strong work ethic, except that it didn't demonstrate an affinity for the type of job for which she was applying.

Once Kelly left the interview room, Davis turned to Jack. "Immediate thoughts?"

Jack looked up from his notes. "A quality candidate for sure. But, in the end, I don't think she saw this position as fit, nor did I. When we got to that scenario where you tried talking her out of the job ... Well, I think you succeeded."

Davis nodded. "You're right I think neither party saw this being a good fit and that's a good thing. It is much better if one or both parties figure that out before being hired."

"That's for sure." Jack's stomach rumbled. "Doing all these interviews sure made me hungry. You ready to eat?"

"Definitely. Why don't we grab our notes and get a quick bite? Then we can go over our morning interviews in more detail."

They went to the student cafeteria and found a table. After they got their food, Jack put his tablet off to one side and arranged his selections on one side of his tray, his coffee and food wrappers on the other.

Davis started laughing. "Are you eating lunch?"

Jack blushed. "Sorry, I'm a little OCD and I've got my habits."

"As long as it doesn't filter into your hiring process," Davis said with a smile. "Remember you don't want an entire team of people who only play third base. Diversity pays off—in more ways than one."

Wow, Jack thought as he looked at his tray. He hadn't even realized what he was doing. He would have to work hard to keep his habits in perspective.

Davis asked his last follow-up question about the middle candidate they saw and turned the page. "Kelly." Davis pointed to Jack's tablet. "What about our last candidate?

Jack shook his head. "My first impression was a little underwhelming. When I went to get her, I waited as she finished up a game she was playing on her phone. I asked if she'd had a busy morning and she said not really. Then I asked if she was taking any interesting classes this semester. She said her two favorites were Zombies in Popular Media and Shakespeare's impact on American literature. When she saw me smile, she said that she loved to watch movies and read."

Davis nodded. "Looking at the rest of her resume and her timeline, I see someone whose experiences reflect what we saw this morning. She is sharp, smart, and consistently gravitates towards activities that avoid a lot of facetime with customers and colleagues. I don't see any evidence to suggest she has interests or natural skillsets that would point her toward Omega."

"Definitely a candidate worth interviewing and maybe a great employee—but for a different organization and a different position. Hiring her for this job would be a disservice to her and Omega. We don't want to put a candidate in a job outside of her vocation and where she won't be happy. This position's not a good fit for her."

"It's not so much about feeling happy as it is feeling fulfilled and engaged. When employees don't feel they are using their talents and aptitudes they feel restless and find little joy in their job. That, of course, affects their productivity and performance." Davis crumpled his napkin and flipped it onto his tray. "We want the right fit because it's costly to get it wrong. HR figures it costs around $200,000 to fully outfit, train and prepare a new employee. We both know what happens when we make a wrong decision."

Jack let out a long sigh. "That's happened to me three times in less than two years. My turnover is costing the company a lot of money and me a lot of sleep." He'd hate to know the true numbers, he thought as he pushed his plate aside. "If I don't turn this around, it will affect my career and drive me crazy."

Now he understood why Carol had pushed him to shadow Davis. It wasn't a grudge or punishment. She was doing him a favor. The hiring process these days seems harder than ever, and he had a lot to learn. The time with his new mentor was already paying off.

"Getting the interview process wrong yields two basic scenarios," Davis continued. "One, the employee quits after floundering for months or longer. Then we go through the process again, doubling the costs to the company. And we haven't even factored in the opportunity costs for the time sourcing candidates—reviewing and weeding out resumes, phone interviews, live interviews, follow-up, background, and reference checks …"

Jack grinned. "Or the lack of productivity during their tenure. You don't have to convince me. If I hadn't already eaten, I'd have lost my appetite. What's the second scenario?"

"Even worse. In the second, the new hire, who isn't right for the job, likes the pay, company car, and benefits and decides to stay. That means we spend a lot of time and effort trying to coach him up or out. And if work ethic is the shortcoming—"

"He probably won't change," Jack interjected. "Because it's a non-teachable quality. A candidate either has it or not and it's why you spend so much time on identifying it."

Davis smiled widely. "Either you're a good student or I'm a great teacher. Well done. Jack, there is an additional cost I was going to mention, if work ethic is a shortcoming then what happens to the work not completed or completed poorly?"

Jack thought for a second as he organized his trash. "Someone else has to do it."

"And that builds resentment by those who are picking up the slack. If a manager doesn't resolve the issue quickly it can produce and lead to bigger problems. You'll have good employees leave."

Jack sat silently. Those words fell heavy on his shoulders. He hadn't considered the burden he had unknowingly placed on his team. He looked up concerned. "I need to thank a few folks who have stepped in to fill the gaps. I've got some great people on my team."

The alarm on Davis' watch chimed. "Let's put this away and see if our next candidate is early."

Making Sure It's a Good Fit:

1. When interviewing candidates, it's important to strike a balance between being cordial and keeping an emotional distance:
   - One of the difficult tasks of a manager is to keep our emotions in check. When we first meet a candidate, we will always form an opinion based on our gut instincts. Whether that opinion is good or bad, we must keep that first impression in check and not let it cloud the rest of the interview.
   - Interviewing is difficult because a manager finds herself passing judgment on a candidate. If she is not careful, she can let her empathy distort her judgment. I've been in situations where I wanted to, 'give this candidate a shot' or I thought maybe this time I'll let my concern about an issue slide because I really like someone. If we let our emotions drive the decision-making process, we may do both ourselves and the candidate a disservice.
   - Bringing a candidate into your organization who isn't a fit will have ripple effects which may lead to bigger problems such as poor team morale, decreased productivity, having good employees leave, and a tarnishing of our reputation. Good employees leave because they don't want to pick up the slack of an underperforming employee and they become discouraged when they see problems that management won't address or solve.

2. If you want to determine fit, meet the candidate:
   - Each candidate you meet will already know most of the questions you are going to ask. Their answers have probably been thought out and even rehearsed. So, getting to know the real candidate is important and that is why starting off with a broad open-ended question or scenario like Davis' helps get the conversation started.
   - Once the conversation is started and the candidate begins to tell his story, hopefully, he will relax, and you can see and hear a more genuine representation. Keep in mind we are not trying to 'trick' the candidate into anything we are just trying to get to know him so that we can make a great decision for both parties.

3. Evaluating a candidate's past experiences will help give insights to his or her strengths:
   - In the example in this chapter, Kelly was worthy of an interview because she was a good student who was had strong work experience. However, the interview confirmed that her overall

interests, activity, experiences showed evidence that she is not a good fit for this job description.

- Kelly's interests, passions, and choices are indicators of the direction in which her abilities and skills ought to draw her. That's why looking at a prospect's transcript and list of extracurricular activities is key. They provide clues as to where she may naturally gravitate.
- Asking probing and follow-up questions will often lead to important clues about her interests and how she makes decisions. If for example, the candidate is talking about a summer job, ask:
  - o Why she chose that position?
  - o How did she get the interview or the job?
  - o What did she like/dislike about the positions?
  - o What would she change about it if she could?
  - o What was her manager like?
  - o Did her manager's leadership style work for her?

4. Fit is also about management style:
   - When probing about a candidate's experiences ask about his manager, team captain or supervisor. Did he enjoy working under that person's leadership? What type of leadership was it, how would they describe it? How do they like to be coached, and what do they find inspiring or discouraging under different leadership styles?
   - Based on the information you uncover; would this candidate thrive under your leadership?

5. Fit is not just about ability and leadership style:
   - Every organization has a culture. Read more about creating a culture in Chapter 16 Onboarding.
   - Teams within an organization also have a culture. Do you see this candidate thriving on your team and organization's culture? Of course, we want to hire diversity, but need to be mindful that if the candidate's personality and demeanor won't fit the current culture then there will be dissonance. For example, if a candidate's idea of work is a relaxed, casual pace and your culture are fast-paced and a bit rigid, then there is a disconnect and an invitation for strife and friction.

6. A candidate's research about the position indicates a desire for her to find fit:
   - Has the candidate taken time to research the organization, other

than reading a one-page summary found on the company's website.?

- Has the candidate performed an informational interview with an employee in your organization? What did she learn about the company's culture and reputation?
- Has the candidate talked to your competitors? What did she learn about the company's culture and reputation?
- What type of questions did the candidate ask at the end of the interview? Were there any questions about the culture or leadership style?
- A self-aware candidate is going to want to make sure that she is a fit for the position as well.

7. Here are some questions to ask if you're unsure of the candidate's calling or fit:
   - Q. When you picture yourself three years from now, what do you see yourself doing?
     - o If a candidate gives an answer along the lines of, "I hope to be in law school," (true story), when he's interviewing for a sales position with an organization in the hospitality sector, it's time to move to the next candidate. Look for candidates whose vision aligns with the organization's.
     - o There are times we think that once a candidate comes on board she will fall in love with the organization and change her mind about her future. Though that could happen, don't bet that a candidate's goals will change once she comes on board. And if her goals don't change, you'll soon find yourself with the same opening all over again.
   - Q. What about this position appeals most to you and why?
     - o As the candidate answers the question, listen for descriptions that highlight his skills and abilities. Answers that focus mainly on pay, benefits, work hours and location reveal priorities that may not be a good fit since these factors can be easily trumped by another organization.
     - o Listen for answers that highlight how the candidate's talents and abilities can best meet your organization's needs.
     - o Listen for answers that while taking all elements into consideration focus largely on what the candidate feels she can bring to the role, department, and organization. A thorough answer that includes these points shows that the

candidate has researched the job and organization and knows herself well enough to see the touchpoints where the job description and organization matches her skills and abilities.

- Q. What prompted you to pursue the jobs, experiences, fields of study, and activities listed on your resume?
    - o You may want to take each of these questions individually, but the questions and their answers will help provide clues as to how she makes choices, process information, and evaluates opportunities. For example, "After speaking to a few people who worked in a local start-up I decided to take the lower wage because it provided me a better opportunity to develop my marketing skills."
        - Here you see someone who researches before a decision is made. Who understands that there is value in something other than a paycheck. She doesn't mind taking a risk after she has evaluated the pros and cons and she has played her card about where her interests lie.
- Q. What skills and lessons learned from your job, experiences, courses, and activities do you feel are most relevant to the position you're applying for and why?
    - o Pursue this line of reasoning until you see how her choices factored into pointing her toward the career path she is interviewing for.

CHAPTER 8
THE SECOND QUALITY OF WHIM

"It is true that integrity alone won't make you a leader, but without integrity, you will never be one."
- Zig Ziglar

Davis and Jack walked back from the Susque State College cafeteria to Career Services to begin their afternoon interviews.

After waking up his tablet, Jack ran his finger down the list of interviews for the day. "Nate's next." Jack got up and peered down the hall. Nate, their one o'clock, was checking in at the receptionist's desk. The candidate glanced at his watch with approval and tightened up his tie. Jack ducked back in the interview room and looked at the clock. "The only thing better than being on time is being early. I'll give him a moment to gather himself and go get him."

As the introductions were made, Nate was fumbling with his files. To break the ice, Davis began with his signature question. He finished the scenario with his usual request. "So, take me through your senior year of high school up to today."

Nate shifted in his seat and began faltering through a description of the events of his senior year. Then he jumped ahead to his first semester of college.

As Nate spoke, Davis looked at his timeline. Davis raised his hand signaling Nate to stop. "Let's back up to the summer before your first semester of college. You worked during those months, right?"

Nate scratched his head. "Oh, yes, right. I worked in the finance department of Guilford Sporting Goods."

"Wow—the finance department," Jack affirmed. "Sounds like a lot of responsibility."

"Actually, it was a pretty sweet job," Nate said. "I helped with deposits and payroll, more importantly, it paid well."

"Nice. So how did you get the job?"

Nate shifted again. "Well, my dad owns the company."

"What's better than knowing someone on the inside?" Davis smiled. "How many hours a week did you work?"

"About ten to fifteen."

Davis continued his queries to try and draw Nate out, but Nate's short, non-descript answers lead to a lot of awkward silence.

Davis looked at the timeline. "What about the Young Entrepreneurs Club?" Davis prompted. "What role did you play there?"

"We met once a month at the Rotary Club and discussed successful start-ups and how a small business is run. We also had local business owners address the group."

Jack made a note and looked to Davis for permission. "Which presentation made the biggest impact on you?"

Nate shifted in his seat. "I don't really recall any one presentation that stood out—I only made a few of the meetings."

Given Nate's answer and based on an educated guess, Davis took Nate's college transcript from his file and probed a bit further. "Tell me about your most difficult course in college."

Nate thought for a second. "Statistics, my junior year."

"How would you rate your performance in the class relative to your peers?" Davis continued. "And why was it so tough?"

Nate's smile was faint. "In relation to my peers, I'd say I was in the top of the bottom third of the class."

Davis paused. "That's a D, right?"

"Well, yes, but the class was big. And the professor wasn't very good. The teaching assistant wasn't too helpful either—poor communication skills."

Davis made a note and looked at Jack who was leaning in to ask a follow-up question.

"We've all had tough courses and professors," Jack agreed. "Mine was information systems, sophomore year. Out of curiosity, when did your course meet?"

"Eight o'clock, Monday, Wednesday and Friday."

"The dreaded eight o'clock. I remember those." Jack smiled. "They can be hard to get to, especially when it's a subject you don't enjoy."

"You said it! And I definitely missed a few of those classes. You know how it is." Nate laughed nervously. "But I always got the notes from my roommate."

Davis put Nate's transcript back in his file. "Okay, now let's think ahead a little. When you picture yourself as a successful businessperson, do you see yourself in the position you're interviewing for and in this industry?"

Taken aback by the frankness of the question, Nate struggled to regain his composure. "Well, I don't have any experience that relates to what you do. But I have a friend with the same type of job as this and he likes it. I think I'd like to give it a try."

Davis and Jack listened to Nate's answers to the remaining questions then Davis checked the time. "Okay, well, do you have any questions for us?"

Nate made a few vague inquiries. The generality of his questions about the position and the organization, along with his lack of inquiries about the department and the market, all indicated that he had done little research on the company before the interview. Davis wrapped up the interview and thanked Nate for his time. Nate left, closing the door behind him.

The room was silent for a moment. "Wow, that just got harder as the interview went on." Jack shook his head. "And it seemed to go on forever."

"Yet he looked good on paper," Davis noted. "Plus, he had some good qualities. Did anything, in particular, stand out during the interview?"

"More than one thing stood out. The first was that great job in the finance department of what turned out to be his dad's company and that Nate only worked ten or fifteen hours a week. And that was during the summer when, according to his timeline, he wasn't taking classes or working another job. In fact, when I saw that job on his resume it looked and read like a fulltime job. Had you not asked about the hours he worked; I would have just assumed he worked fulltime."

Jack looked at his list. "Then there was the Entrepreneurs Club. Seemed like Nate only joined because it would look good on his resume. Some candidates are motivated to join a club to round out their resume. That's fine as long as they're involved. But that clearly wasn't the case here. The only thing Nate had mentioned was the speakers and he didn't even say much about them. Overall, he didn't sound too invested."

Davis nodded. "See, you do have good instincts. Those are good pickups. Now if you had to name the one quality about Nate that concerns you most what would it be?"

"His lack of candor and transparency. His answers were vague like he knew he hadn't been as involved in work or college as he made himself out to be. And it's not that he isn't bright. It's that he wasn't candid about his background. Makes me wonder why he didn't invest more of himself."

"Right," Davis agreed. "That's why I probed more about his grades."

"The top of the bottom third!" Jack said with a laugh. "Now that's one of the best lines I've heard yet. His answers to most of your questions made me wonder how many classes he attended for that 8 o'clock course."

"Precisely, but something else about that bothered me even more. When

Nate referred to the D in stats, he said he'd been 'given' a D, like the responsibility for his low grade, was somebody else's. He wasn't given that D. He earned it. Now imagine what an attitude like that would be like to work with."

Jack winced. He already knew that from past employees. "I hate to think."

Davis smiled. "It's time for the second quality I look for in good hires."

Jack reached for his tablet and navigated to his notes. "It's about time. I'm all ears."

"The second non-negotiable, non-teachable quality is integrity. It's the backbone of trust," Davis affirmed. "If a prospect lacks integrity, how can you trust him to put in a full day's work or submit an accurate expense report or a projected business plan? In the end, you have to wonder if anything he tells you is the truth."

"I know," Jack agreed. "My last boss used to have her assistant tell certain clients she wasn't in even though she was right there in the office. That always bothered me. It got to where every time I was told my boss wasn't there, I wondered if it was a lie." Jack paused. "It didn't take long before I started to wonder if he was telling the truth about anything. In the end, I put in for a transfer to another division and was glad when I left."

Davis nodded and picked up Nate's resume. Jack, you nailed it. As I scan Nate's resume, I wonder what on this is true, untrue or enhanced. When trust has been broken it is very difficult to repair. Davis pushed his chair back and stood up. "One key quality this company needs in its people is integrity—and we can't teach that. It's a quality born out of a person's upbringing and value system."

Jack looked puzzled. "I get it, thou shalt not lie. We learn that as kids. But we're not talking about religion. Are we?"

Davis shook his head. "I define Integrity as a commitment to make the correct moral and ethical decision, even when forces are telling and pulling one to do otherwise. People of faith should have it. But a lot of other people have it too. I do my best to try and live with integrity in all my dealings. You can ask me any question and I'll tell you the truth. Or I'll tell you I can't answer right now. Either way, I won't lie to you."

Jack nodded. "I feel the same way. My family instilled it in me and so did most of my teachers. They wouldn't have had it any other way."

"To be fair to Nate we are all a work in progress and we certainly aren't perfect. We don't know his view on integrity or if he struggles with it," Davis added. "But there were enough red flags during the interview that my gut tells me that we can't ignore them."

Jack nodded. "I understand why integrity made your must-have list. As I sit here and reflect on my past interviews. I can't say that I ever pursued this quality or paid attention to it in an interview. Yet I've seen the damage caused by those who lack it."

"Yes. I call the damage an integrity tax. When a process, person, or organization's integrity is in question it is charged an integrity tax."

"An integrity tax?" said Jack with disdain. "What is it—exactly?"

"Like most taxes, you'll want to avoid this one as well. Let me give you an example. Before the attacks on 9/11, airline travel used to be simpler. I used to catch a taxi, jump out and walk right up to my gate."

"Was security different back then?"

"That's just it. There was no security."

"No security," exclaimed Jack. "How could that be?"

"Jack there were few concerns about people blowing up airplanes or hijacking them and flying them into buildings. It just didn't happen. I mean planes were hijacked but rarely. And it usually ended on a tarmac somewhere after negotiations."

"You mean these complicated scanning systems and TSA lines are new?"

"Yes. And that is the integrity tax I'm referring to. When there is a lack of trust solutions and safeguards must be introduced to protect the innocent parties. This usually adds greater costs and lengthy delays. It's costly to everyone."

Jack slid his tablet towards him and added to his notes. He looked up and let out a sigh. "Ok. I gotta admit. Integrity is a lot more important than I had thought."

Davis smiled. The room fell silent. Davis spun his pen on the table for a moment while he collected his thoughts. "Let me share one additional observation about integrity. People who lack integrity assume other people are the same as they are. They're hard to coach because they figure their managers are cynical, too. And they're hard to work with because others quickly realize that their colleague lacks integrity and can't be trusted."

Jack nodded. "One time when I had to caution my team about upcoming budget constraints, I overheard one person saying to another direct report that I probably got in trouble for going over budget last quarter and now the team was bearing the consequences. Fortunately, I stepped in and corrected his misinformation campaign. Can you imagine the seeds of discord he's been sowing over the years? I've had run-ins with that person and another like him before and now that you have me thinking about integrity—I'm guessing that is at the heart of much of our friction. It didn't take much for them to challenge me like I had a history of stretching the truth. I think in most cases they were thinking of what they would have done, assuming I'd do the same."

Davis's smile was sympathetic. "So, how was the working relationship in those instances?"

"Miserable. In that one case, I never felt like the guy trusted me. Other employees can sense that, too, you know. One bad attitude easily spoils the bunch."

Davis grinned. "That's why we're spending so much time and effort to make sure we hire integrity. Getting this process correct will save everyone, most importantly you, time, energy and angst."

Jack took a look at his notes. "All right. The two non-negotiable, non-teachables so far are work ethic and integrity. And I understand why they're essential. But don't you think we're being a little judgmental? I mean, nobody's perfect and people do change."

Davis nodded. "True. People can learn and develop a more robust work ethic and a deeper commitment to integrity. The key here is, those aren't traits I can teach. I can demonstrate them and encourage them, but I can't teach them to someone. To ensure a great hire, those foundational qualities have to already be established to some degree before they're hired."

"I guess you're right. And as to Nate, I wouldn't pursue him because instinct and experience both tell me he wouldn't be a good fit and he lacks the integrity we're looking for."

"Then we agree," Davis affirmed.

"Good," Jack nodded. "Integrity seems to be on everyone's lips these days. Did you go through the compliance training?"

"I did." Davis tapped the table for emphasis. "There are organizations that have paid hundreds of millions—and, in some cases, billions—of dollars because a few individuals out of the lot didn't have enough integrity. Yes, we can introduce the principles of integrity and reinforce our company's commitment to them, but we can only hope they abide by them. But where possible it's a lot better to hire individuals that can demonstrate integrity."

"There's also another benefit of hiring someone with integrity," Davis added. "Remember I talked about an integrity tax? There is also an integrity premium. The integrity premium gives me the ability to increase my productivity. I have three people I can hand assignments to and know that they'll work with the same care as I would. This not only preserves my credibility; it allows me to work on more urgent issues. And I can do it with focus and confidence, which I couldn't do if I didn't trust those people."

"Great point!" Jack pointed his pen towards Davis. "When I can't trust someone, I find myself micromanaging him. I'm checking up and checking in. I find myself preoccupied with what he is doing or not doing. I know he hates when I micromanage. Heck, I hate when I have to micromanage. It's a lose-lose."

Davis nodded. "Which is why we're taking the time to hire these qualities upfront. Too much is riding on them—the company's reputation, our future and the candidate's, not to mention the working relationships within the department. An employee with integrity multiplies work capacity, whereas a colleague who lacks it handicaps everyone."

A bell chimed on Jack's cell. "Time for our next candidate." He checked his tablet for the name. "Our next interviewee is Brett—a lettered football player with a 2.75 GPA. Gina Stuart from the New York office recommended him." Jack rolled his eyes. "This ought to be good."

Discerning a Candidate's Integrity

1. There are many reasons why integrity is a crucial and non-negotiable quality to look for in a prospective new hire:
    *   First, integrity is the backbone of all relationships—personal and professional. A person who lacks integrity is hard to trust and breeds doubt and suspicion in colleges, customers, and management.
    *   Integrity adds stability to the work environment and to relationships. Integrity gives way to a consistent and predictable work environment since decisions truth and acceptable behavior are not found on a sliding scale.
    *   A manager with integrity will not be capricious in his business and professional dealings, and that makes for a healthy work environment.
    *   Integrity can be modeled, it can be reinforced as a company standard, but it can't be taught and that is why managers must be committed to uncovering it in the interview process.
    *   When an employee's integrity is in question, productivity erodes, and costs rise because other colleagues are covering or checking his work which affects morale and workflow. If an employee eventually has to be terminated for his integrity then the costs skyrocket because the entire hiring, onboarding, and training process must be repeated.

2. There are a number of ramifications of hiring someone who has a weak or suspect view of integrity:
    *   When integrity is in question and trust suspect there is an integrity tax that is imposed upon the relationship or organization. This is the cost of working under the cloud of questionable trust. Double, triple checking, following up, verifying numbers and facts, asking for clarification and second opinions are all examples of an integrity tax; the cost of doing business with an individual or organization which has questionable integrity.
    *   The continual effort needed to verify the work of an employee who lacks integrity wastes the manager's time and energy and those of the employee, not to mention the time, energy, and morale of other employees and colleagues.
    *   Those who lack integrity can cost the company millions of dollars due to dishonest business practices. These costs can come in the

form of litigation, for example, Pfizer had to pay $2.3 billion to the government for marketing one of their products incorrectly. The cost can also come from business that is lost from individuals who no longer want to work with or for your organization.

- Those who lack integrity tend to project their distrust on others, further decreasing productivity and eroding trust. For example, if an employee used to skip our early on Fridays, she falsely may project that on others because that is what she did. This thinking can cause friction and discord.

3. There are several ways to approach an interview to uncover whether a person has integrity:
   - As you move through a candidate's timeline, probe as to why she made job changes or changed her major. There may be useful information that ties in with other areas of the candidate's decision making or ethical challenges.
   - Ask why she chose a job, school, or activity. The stories behind big decisions may offer clues to a firing or an event that encouraged her to leave an unhealthy situation or maybe it was a very natural transition, but it is often in these life events where you may get a glimpse of her integrity.
     o Hint: Revisit these scenarios during the second interview to make sure the stories are consistent.
   - Ask the prospect about her biggest disappointment or failure to see whether she is forthcoming about the situation and whether she takes the appropriate level of responsibility for it.
   - Ask about a difficult decision(s) he had to make and why it was difficult? If he had to make the decision(s) today, would he come to the same conclusions?
   - Look and listen for ethical conflicts in the candidate's decision-making process, the choices that resulted, and ask how the candidate handled these.
   - Ask the prospect targeted questions about your company and the open position to see whether she has done the requisite research. If she has not researched the position or the company deeply enough, can she say so? Though I might be disappointed in her lack of initiative which reflects on her work ethic, I would be impressed with her integrity for being transparent and forthcoming.
   - Look for instances where the candidate was given increasing degrees of responsibility during her career or schooling. Though not definitive, candidates who consistently are given greater degrees of responsibility are seen as trustworthy and honest. Most

organizations would not give more responsibility to someone whose integrity was in question.

- Ask a candidate about a poor performance review, or his last performance review and any areas he fell below expectations. Did he agree with those conclusions? Why or why not?
- If the candidate is just a few years out of college, ask about his worst grade or class. What made it so terrible and what factors lead to his poor grade. Look for some ownership and transparency in his answer.
- Ask the candidate what piece(s) of advice he has been given that he has found most useful and why?

4. Here are some key benefits to hiring an employee with integrity.
- As much as a trust tax will cost your organization, there is a trust premium that will multiply your and your team's efforts.
- Because they can be trusted, there is little need for micro-managing which frees up your time and emotions.
- You have an assurance that they are dealing with internal and external clients fairly, which reflects well on you and your team.
- Employees with integrity are accountable.
- They won't be stealing or taking shortcuts.
- Their integrity is contagious. When others hear their accountability and honesty it inspires others to do likewise.

Defining Terms:
- Integrity: A commitment to do what is right, even when other forces are telling and pulling one to do otherwise. This quality is developed early in life and becomes part of a person's personal makeup.
- In short: The ethical response.
- Accountability: Closely tied to integrity, it is the willingness to own one's successes and failures. For instance, Nate didn't "own" the grade he earned. A lack of accountability is cause for concern.

CHAPTER 9
SURPRISED

"Character cannot be developed in ease and quiet. Only through
experience of trial and suffering can the soul be strengthened,
ambition inspired, and success achieved."
-Helen Keller

It has been a full afternoon and there was just one interview left. Jack
reached for the last resume and timeline, Brett, a star football player with a
2.75 GPA. "In my experience students who focused on sports for most of
their high school and college years focused on little else. But I suppose if
Gina Stuart recommended him, we have to at least take the time to
interview him."

"Now let's not rush to judgment," Davis cautioned. "And let's
remember the drill—get him talking. My other rule of thumb with
icebreakers is to ask one of two questions. If the interview is before noon
on Wednesday, I ask what they did last weekend. If it's after one p.m. on
Wednesday, I ask what they're planning to do this weekend."

"I like it," Jack said as he went to the door. "It's simple, which means I
can remember it. Wonder what a star athlete is doing this weekend ..." His
voice trailed off as he went out into the hall.

A few minutes later Jack's infectious laughter echoed in the hallway then
Jack and Brett came into the office. Brett's six-four-inch frame and solid
250 pounds nearly filled the room. He had 'defensive tackle' written all over
him. His nearly shaved head and goatee made him a bit intimidating, but his
broad smile softened the look. Davis wondered whether Brett's personality
matched his appearance and how that would mesh with Omega's
conservative customer base, He shook his head no, he thought, he needed

to be careful not to let his preconceptions take over. He'd have to balance his instincts with insight.

Reviewing Brett's timeline again, Davis saw that Brett had played varsity football in high school and college but had missed playing his junior year of high school and sophomore year of college. Davis looked again at the transcript, then at the timeline. Both he and Jack had missed the gaps, Davis thought. He quickly calculated that it had taken Brett nine semesters to graduate college, and it looked like he'd had to pull out for a semester because of grades, which would explain his not playing football sophomore year. Davis felt like kicking himself for missing such obvious red flags. Jack was right. The interview would be a waste of time.

Once the introductions were done, instead of asking his usual start-up question, Davis decided to speed the interview up.

"Well, Brett, I see you played football and you have a couple of big rings on your fingers. Looks like you went to a few bowl games. Congratulations."

Brett lifted his hand and smiled. "I have to admit, I'm pretty proud of these."

Life gets a little more complicated than winning bowl games, thought Davis. "I was wondering if you could explain a few gaps in your resume for me. I see you missed a year of football in high school and again in college. And according to the transcript, it seems to have taken you an additional semester to graduate." Davis glanced at Jack and saw him looking quickly at the timeline then the transcript and making notes. I guess he missed the red flags, too, Davis thought.

Brett shifted in his chair. "I don't know if I should say this, but it'll probably come out eventually." The room fell silent as if everyone on campus had stopped talking. Brett turned his head and pointed to a horseshoe-shaped scar. "This is from brain surgery."

For the next twenty minutes, Davis and Jack sat transfixed as Brett described a unique medical condition that had required half-dozen major surgeries over the years, explaining the time he had missed in high school and college.

"Wow, that's some story," said Davis. "I'm amazed you were able to play football at all."

"Being in great shape helped me bounce back faster than any patient the doctors had seen with this condition," Brett boasted. "But for me being healthy is a way of life, by necessity."

His quiet smile made it seem he'd just described a last-second championship play, Jack thought. But it was clear from how Brett told his story that victory over personal obstacles was what meant the most to him.

With the few minutes that remained, Davis looked over Brett's timeline and focused on a few of his other experiences. Brett was easy to talk to and transparent in his answers, and he had a great sense of humor.

As the meeting drew to a close, Davis turned to Jack. "So, what's Brett doing this weekend?"

Jack recalled the earlier conversation, looked at Brett. "You're going down to—Maryland, right?" Jack turned to Davis. "All I know is that he loves crab cakes as much as I do," Jack said with a grin.

"That's right," Brett said with a smile. "And I am going down to Bethesda. But it's not for fun. I'll be at the National Institutes of Health to get my yearly checkup," Brett said with a smile.

Davis shook his head. "I don't get it, Brett. You've had the deck stacked against you most of your life. You didn't get to play ball all the years you wanted to, you missed school, missed out on social events and a good portion of your teenage years. You didn't even get to graduate college with your friends. If anyone has reason to gripe about life, it's you." Davis paused. "I don't get a sense of that from you at all."

Brett smiled. "Gripe? About what? The way I see it, I've had a good life. And I've enjoyed every minute of it—well, almost," he added with a grin. Then he grew serious. "My dad was a helicopter pilot in Afghanistan, and he's seen everything. Most things he doesn't talk about, but he knows what it means to serve and always taught us, kids, to value every day. And when we hit one of life's bumps in the road, we need to think of them not as potholes but as launching pads."

Jack smiled. "What a great perspective. Your dad shared a valuable gift with you."

"And I figure, I am who I am because of what I've been through." Brett pointed to his scar. "I count my scars as blessings, A lot of kids I've gone to school with get bent out of shape over little things, but I'm thrilled to be alive. That makes a lot of things easier to face."

Davis reached into his messenger bag and handed Brett an information packet. "Do me a favor and look this over."

"Your First Career Choice May Be Your Best," Brett read. "Thanks. I'll look forward to reading it."

Davis nodded. "Omega prides itself on developing emerging talent into professionals. We also train our people to be leaders. You're already on your way. With Omega, you'll have the tools to succeed because we'll provide them. I'd like to schedule another interview for next week, same time. Can you make it?"

"That would be great." Brett smiled. "It will be something to look forward to over the weekend."

Davis grinned. "Perfect. I'll be in touch with the logistics."

Brett shook hands with both men, thanked each for his time, and left.

Once Brett was out of the room Davis got up and paced in front of the window.

"Something wrong?" Jack asked.

Davis shook his head. "I'm annoyed with myself."

"Why?" Jack looked surprised. "Brett turned out to be a great candidate."

Davis let out a long sigh and checked his cell. "Let's spend a few minutes gathering our thoughts for the day."

☐

How Candidates Respond to Obstacles and How We Respond to Candidates Matters

1. Exploring a struggle, difficult time, or obstacle a candidate has faced tells the interviewer two things:
   - First, the exploration tells the interviewer how the candidate views obstacles. Does he see them as:
     o A launchpad toward growth and opportunity
     o The reason he never achieved his full potential
     o Part of life's ups and downs
     o A reason for bitterness and anger or as an opportunity in disguise
   - Second, the exploration tells the interviewer how the candidate responds to obstacles. Does she see it as:
     o A challenge to be overcome
     o An opportunity to be used for good, such as starting a support group, or raising funds for a charity or solving an unmet need he uncovered during this event.
     o A situation that has led to bitterness or resentment. Be careful because these attitudes will spill over into the workplace

2. Here are questions that can help draw out a candidate's perspective on personal obstacles:
   - What event (positive or negative) has most affected you? Why?
   - What would you say is the most difficult experience you've encountered so far? Why is this so?
   - What one event has helped shape you into who you are today?
     o What did you learn from this event—how did it affect you?
   - What do you do differently now as a result of this? (Listen for how the candidate answers the question to determine whether she sees challenges as opportunities or obstacles to personal progress and growth.)
   - If you went through those circumstances again, what would you do differently?
   - Would you be willing to go through the hardship again if given the chance?
     o Remember that hardship is relative to each person—what matters is the candidate's response to challenges.

    o   What you are listening for is a candidate who realizes that they are the strong resourceful person because of what life's difficulties have taught them. You want to hear that hardships have made them better not bitter.

3. If you'd like to see how a candidate might respond to a challenge, find a discrepancy on their timeline or something that is not clear and push for details.

    • You'd want to hear someone who welcomes correction and sees a verbal challenge as an opportunity to clear up a misunderstanding.

    • Listen for a defensiveness.

    • This series of questions is not an invitation to be annoying or exasperating. It should be a natural, calm exchange. I've seen interviewers bait candidates into a confrontational exchange and then claim that they wanted to see how they responded. I don't believe you will get an accurate picture of how a frustrated candidate will respond because an interview is a very unnatural setting.

        o   Remember, the candidate is evaluating you as well, so be kind and reasonable.

4. To explore your own preconceived notions in the context of candidate interviews, consider what personality type you find hardest to deal with:

    • Why is this case? What are some examples from your prior experience that factor into your perspective?

    • How do you deal with this personality type now?

        o   How can you grow in your approach to difficult personalities?

5. Remember to listen to the interviewee's full story, especially for these considerations:

    • Does the candidate engage those listening in her story? Does she draw you into her story, and does she speak with thoughtful consideration of the circumstances and lessons learned?

    • One reason to consider how a candidate tells his story is that if he can't relay it candidly and with maturity, he may have difficulties telling your organization's story.

    • Put yourself in the position of your customer or as a fellow colleague; would this interviewee be someone you wanted to give your time, attention or business to.

CHAPTER 10
THE THIRD QUALITY

You might not be able to control your circumstances, but you
can control your response to your circumstances.
-Condoleezza Rice

Jack finished recording Davis' comments on Stuart, the fourth candidate of the afternoon. "All right, the home stretch. Let's take the last few minutes and tackle Brett." He looked at Jack. "Let me ask a question. What were your initial thoughts when you saw Brett was a football player and had missed several seasons and graduated late?"

Jack shrugged. "I thought he was the stereotypical jock who was ineligible to play because of low grades." Jack hesitated. "And I figured the interview would be a waste of time."

Davis nodded. "I felt the same." He shook his head. "We let our instincts take over, piled our prejudices on top and made some snap assumptions. I know better than to let my instincts go unchallenged. If I had rushed that interview like I wanted to, we might not have gotten to know what a great young man Brett is. He saved himself by being open and honest. It's a good lesson."

Jack nodded thoughtfully. "You're right. I initially wrote him off. I like him a lot, too, and not just for his personality. It takes dedication and discipline to be a competitive varsity football player and bounce back the way he did after all those surgeries."

Davis sat down. "And even with all that working against him, I only saw one class that he struggled in. All-in-all he still kept his grades up, stayed focused and excelled." Davis looked at his notes. "So based on the job description and what we know of the organization, how does Brett stack up?"

Jack tapped his tablet. "Work ethic—well, he's certainly got that. As far as integrity goes—I was impressed that he was so open with us. He didn't have to be, and he never leaned on his condition as an excuse for any shortcomings on or off the field." Jack circled "integrity." "I definitely think he has integrity."

Davis smiled. "I agree. So, are you ready for the third secret to hiring great talent?"

Jack swiped his tablet and navigated to the section he had facetiously titled, "The Longest Way to Hire on a Whim." He tapped the screen. "Is this also a non-negotiable and non-teachable?"

"Absolutely!" Davis grinned. "The third secret to hiring great talent is—hire maturity."

Jack started to enter "maturity" then stopped. "Just so we're clear, do you mean maturity as in age? Because I don't think that age on its own is an accurate indicator of how mature a person is."

Davis smiled. "Good point. But what I mean is something different—that there are two basic ways people mature. The first is that they grow older and more mature because they've lived longer than other people. The other way is when life and its challenges season them and they allow their experiences to be a catalyst for growth."

Jack nodded. "I agree. I know people who have gone through problems, not all as severe as Brett's, but still pretty tough times. And not all of them allowed their experiences to work for them, help them grow, as you say. Which means we're not just looking for candidates who've had a difficult life or faced obstacles, right?"

"Right. Because sometimes when people go through problems or face obstacles the experience has the opposite effect." Davis smiled. "For simplicity sake, you might say each person has a choice when going through a trial, they can become bitter or better. The first group sees obstacles in a completely negative way, as having no redeeming value whatsoever, just a raw deal handed out by some celestial card dealer or an unfair break that keeps working against them. Do you know how to recognize them?"

Jack nodded. "I think I know what you mean. The people who get bitter see setbacks as continually working against them. They make excuses for why they're not where they should be or want to be in their job or personal life. It reminds me of something I heard the motivational speaker Zig Ziglar talk about. These people often use words like shoulda, woulda, and coulda."

"Exactly. Along with their propensity for making excuses they usually have another response. They reject any possible good coming from their experience. And they hang onto that attitude in work and life. You can't always see it but you sure can see and hear its effect—it comes out as bitterness. It's like a weed and the roots grow deep and are a real deterrent to growth because it infects the way they think and process. Life is seen through the lens of all that they were robbed of instead of what life's difficulties have taught them. The mature person doesn't ask, 'why is this happening to me, but what can I learn from this?

Jack sat back in his chair. "I hadn't thought of it that way. But it makes sense that if a candidate makes excuses for why life hasn't worked out for her, she'll poison the atmosphere for everyone else. I've worked with a few of those. It's rough."

Davis nodded. "That's why I steer clear of hiring those individuals. They're not only hard to work with, but they're also hard to coach. When they can't complete a project or reach a quota, it's always someone else's fault. It's as if there's a built-in immunity to learning something more about themselves."

Jack sat forward. "Then Brett is definitely in the other category of people, those who can see their hardships as opportunities to learn, grow, to make them better. He has—" Jack looked down at his tablet, "maturity."

"Right," Davis agreed. "Instead of just suffering through the difficulties people like him choose to embrace them and grow."

"It is a tall order and takes time and perspective. To think that Brett could look upon his circumstances and still be grateful."

"You've touched on one of my favorite words—gratitude. It's a beautiful emotion to see and hear. Now watch this." Davis held his hands up and as if he was drawing to items together, "I've always seen the word gratitude as a combination of the words great and attitude—gratitude."

"I never saw that before. I love it and I'm going to steal it."

Davis smiled, "It's all yours. Maturity can be found in the foundation of some of history's most important figures. These men and women used their hardships to spur them on to greatness. People like Abraham Lincoln, Rosa Parks, Ben Carson, and the great Olympian Louis "Louie" Zamperini. If you want inspiration and to gain a perspective, read their stories."

"I read the book, Unbroken. What a breathtaking story. I kept asking myself, when is he going to give up? And to think of the man he became— amazing." Jack paused as he sighed deeply. "I guess the way people react to pressure says a lot."

"Right," Davis said with a nod. "So, when we see a young man like Brett, who has every reason to be bitter but views resentfulness as a foreign concept, it's a beautiful thing. That attitude can spread through a department, too, and for the betterment of everyone."

Jack smiled. "Sharon's the same. As someone from a big family, she had to work hard to get through high school and college. But she didn't see it as a personal hardship, more like part of life. I didn't hear any resentment or regret. I think she even used the words—" Jack scrolled back through his notes. "I'm better off for it."

"Now you're getting the hang of it," Davis agreed. "Which proves that maturity, the third pillar, is vital. When hardships come at work and they will—deadlines, customers who repeatedly say no, friction among coworkers and with the boss—mature employees are better able to process and handle those situations. They can even inspire others to deal with them better, the way Brett did with us. Look at what Brett's been through. Do you think a customer saying no a bunch of times or a colleague getting in his face will rattle Brett's cage? For him, difficult customers and colleagues won't be life-shattering experiences. He'll put events like this in their proper perspective and move on."

Jack nodded. "And if Sharon has to work late or over a weekend, I don't imagine she'll whine about hard work."

"They're both great examples," Davis affirmed. "When you hire maturity, you hire colleagues who tend to have more measured responses to what others might see as a crisis or difficult circumstances."

"When one person might panic, the mature person keeps his cool."

"Now you are getting to the heart of why it is important to hire maturity. It's not just if someone might panic, it's bigger than that. When you have individuals who have learned from hardships, listen up Jack this is key. They tend to express the right emotion, at the right intensity, for the right reason. Mature people tend not to get angry when provoked, become fearful when bad news hits, or get offended when insulted. Their life experiences help regulate their responses to what might be emotional triggers for others."

"That is fascinating. I've worked with angry people before. It is miserable. Everyone walks on eggshells. I didn't feel like I could challenge him on the quality of his work. We all just kind of avoided him. It's interesting," Jack mused. "Sharon and Brett seemed more poised than some of the seasoned people I've had on my team." He tapped his pen. "This interviewing and active listening—it's tough stuff. I'm really going to have to step up my game if I'm going to identify and hire maturity."

"Eighty percent of the work of interviewing is knowing what to look and listen for," Davis agreed. "But let me give you one other clue that might help in your effort to identify maturity—emotional intelligence."

Jack grinned. "I've heard of it—Carol's a big fan."

"I can understand why," Davis affirmed. "Emotional intelligence is related to emotional maturity. Colleagues with a high level of emotional intelligence have the ability to interpret and control their own emotions and to recognize and react appropriately to the emotions of others. Maturity and emotional intelligence go hand in hand."

"Makes sense and I can see why maturity made the list." Jack looked at his notes. "So that's it? The Three Qualities Needed to Hire the Best, by Davis Walker."

Davis laughed. "Our work is done here. Let's gather up our materials and leave this place better than we found it. I think we're almost there." Davis zippered his messenger style bag and waved to Jack. "Walk with me. I'd like to grab a cup of tea for the ride home."

Discerning a Candidate's Maturity

1. As a review, consider why maturity is important to hire in a candidate:
   - Maturity signals that the candidate will be better prepared to handle a stressful or emotional situation with the proper, measured response.
   - Maturity also shows that the prospect will look at obstacles and problems as learning opportunities, not just difficulties to be endured.
   - Maturity in a candidate projects internal consistency and brings emotional stability to the prospect's coworkers, department, and managers.
   - Candidates with emotional intelligence possess resolve and resilience. They can process and react to stress, pressure, and uncertainty with a calmer, more thoughtful approach than those who lack maturity. In today's dynamic workplace, maturity is an essential quality to hire and retain.

2. Here are a few questions to ask your candidates to reveal their maturity level:
   - When you picture yourself professionally in three years from now, what does the picture look like? (Listen for whether the scenario is mature and realistic.)
   - What personalities do you have the most difficult time dealing with? Why?
   - Do you have specific examples of a difficult person you've worked with? How did you cope with their attitude or personality? Did the relationship ever get better? Why?
   - Can you give me an example of a person who you have chosen to avoid and why? Look for the discernment to identify personalities that are toxic and immature. If he can identify the lack of maturity in another, it is often because he values it in himself.

3. When you ask the following types of questions, listen for how the candidate responds to life's problems and for how he or she embraces these events:
   - What event (good or bad) most affected your life? Why?
   - What would you say is the most difficult experience you've ever had and why?
   - What are some of your pet peeves—what frustrates you most and why? (Listen for whether these are mature or immature issues.)

- Describe your best-ever experience—whether in work, school, or life. When was it, and why was it important to you?
- Do you learn best from your mistakes or someone else's mistakes? Can you give me an example of both? (Learning from both is important. What you want to hear is that they learn from mistakes.)

4. Ask the candidate about one of his great regrets in life and why he views it as such:
   - Don't' judge the regret, like life's difficulties they are relative to each individual. Listen for a root of bitterness or complaining and listen to see whether there is recognition of an opportunity for growth.
   - What did he learn, and if the situation were to arise again, what would he do differently this time and why?

5. Since emotional intelligence is a key character trait closely related to maturity, it's important to explore this trait with the candidate:
   - Describe a specific, emotionally charged situation and how she responded it to it and why she chose that approach.

6. Here are some key benefits to hiring an employee with maturity.
   - They are a stabilizing factor to your team. They tend to control their emotions and tend not to tolerate other's inappropriate responses to stress.
   - They are cooler under pressure and can help regulate the team's response during a crisis.
   - They tend not to be gossipers or ones to pass along rumors. They go one step further, they thwart gossip.
   - Because they can control their emotions, they remain clear thinking and are able to be solution-oriented when problems or setbacks arise.
   - They are better able to hear and positively respond to constructive feedback.

Defining Term:
- Maturity: Wisdom born out of life events that gives individuals the ability to express the right emotion at the right intensity for the situation, along with the discernment to interpret other's emotions.
- In short: A measured response.

CHAPTER 11
ONE MORE ESSENTIAL QUALITY

"Experience is not what happens to you; it is what you do
with what happens to you."
-Aldous Huxley

Davis opened the door to the breakroom and held it for Jack. "Remember I said there were three secrets? I lied."

"Looks like someone has a problem with Integrity!" Jack said with a smile.

"Relax. Put your red flag away. This is the quality that unites all the traits and it's essential to hire."

"And like the others, we need to hire it because we can't teach it?"

"Right," Davis affirmed. "Jack. A cup of coffee for the road?"

Jack looked puzzled. "Sure, but what's the trait?"

Davis smiled. "Any ideas? Care to take a guess," he queried, handing Jack his coffee.

"I've been wondering. What about being a self-starter. You know, initiative. Is it something like that?"

Davis grinned. "Good guess but that would fall under work ethic. Let me help you out. The last one is humility."

Jack took the cup. "What about humility is so great it's worked its way to Davis Walker's must-have list? You certainly don't want hires to be shy or quiet—that doesn't sound like anyone you'd hire."

Davis shook his head. "Humility doesn't mean someone who always takes a backseat—think of it as the opposite of proud." He said as he stirred his tea.

"But I've always believed people should take pride in their work and in themselves," Jack noted.

"Great insight Jack. The elements you just described are the positive side of pride, but there is another side of pride that humility keeps in check. I define a humble person as someone who's willing and able to be taught and corrected, a person who knows he or she hasn't 'arrived' yet." Davis put his tea on the table. "Have you ever tried to teach someone who knows everything?"

"Only every time my son brings me his math homework."

"Good example. He lacks that humility and you can't help him until he's ready to learn."

"Okay, I think I get the picture." Jack raised his cup. "And thanks for the coffee. But we're looking to hire tomorrow's leaders. I'm not sure how humility fits with that goal."

"I'd argue that humility is one of the most important qualities, if not the most important, to have in a leader. I wouldn't follow somebody who didn't possess and express humility. Think back to the leaders you most respect."

Jack sipped his coffee. "Come to think of it. In my experience, I'd much rather work for a manager who is open to feedback and always looking to grow and learn. If I could avoid working for the one who always must be the smartest person in the room, I would. I don't work well under that type of leadership. I like this quality. The ability to be humble—humbility." Jack joked.

"Very clever Jack; humility and ability, they should go together. We want to hire those who can lead and follow. People who are open to new ideas, perspectives and who are looking to grow and learn—that's the attitude we want to bring into Omega."

"I can see why this is such a valuable quality to pursue."

"As a manager, there is one other aspect of humility that I appreciate. Humble people generally take criticism well and they can be coached because they don't let their pride get in the way of correction and advice. It is an impossible and maddening task to try and coach someone who doesn't want to learn or change. What is most depressing to me is when I realize I have an employee who has made the choice to stop growing and investing in themselves. They are now a liability to me."

Davis sipped his tea and continued. "In essence, we're looking for the candidate who for example during a performance review has the attitude of 'Skip the niceties—what can I do to become better?' We want somebody who's enthusiastic about improving and doesn't view feedback and advice from managers and peers as a personal insult. That's somebody who knows he doesn't have all the answers and that's a person you can coach."

Jack put down his coffee. "You know, I've mentored dozens of new colleagues and everything you're saying rings true. I've managed both types of employees. Those who wanted to be better and who were open to coaching and those who would take a defensive posture whenever I had an opportunity to provide some constructive feedback. After listening to you define humility, I'm betting that was the difference between the two. It's ironic—the employees with the most pride seem to have the frailest egos."

"Right. And it's that kind of pride that strains both our teams and our productivity. A lack of humility tends to manifest as a personality who's inflexible, argumentative and divisive. An attitude like that can erode the continuity of the team and hinder progress pretty quickly. He's the guy who breeds discontentment by complaining about process, the company, and management."

"Wow. I know just the type you are describing, and they are painful to work with." Jack said with a nod. "But what about someone who's skilled at his job or in a particular role and knows it?"

"Good question," Davis agreed. "So, let's not confuse confidence with pride. For example, the great basketball player, Steve Curry didn't come across as proud, just somebody who was sure of himself and confident based on his past performance and abilities. He also had his talent confirmed by other people, his coach, teammates, fans—"

"I get it. Confidence is based on confirmation, like a proven track record, for example. Which is why it's so frustrating to work with people who are confident, overconfident really, but have little to no history or evidence to back it up. And it helps when some of that validation comes from outside sources," Davis said with a grin.

"I can see why discovering and hiring humility is important." Jack paused. "And I think I'm finally starting to appreciate your interviewing approach, especially if it helps preserve my team." He chucked his cup in the trash and yawned. "It's amazing—the candidates do all the talking but I'm the one who's exhausted."

"Active listening is hard work," Davis answered. "Especially when the clues we're looking for are small and nuanced."

"I'll say," Jack said, stretching. "I'm ready to go, you? He got up and opened the door. "You know maybe it's not all their fault. We have several generations in the workforce who grew up getting participation trophies. They spent their childhood hearing how wonderful they are and that most of their accomplishments were great. Those tactics may have protected and built up their self-esteem while they were young, but some have yet to transition over to reality where true performance and contributions are what makes a person valuable to their organization."

"And growing up in an environment where everybody's the best or the most valuable player makes those accolades meaningless. Which means that a number of candidates have a skewed sense of their abilities and self-worth."

Jack paused and looked at Davis. "And yet, we met several outstanding candidates today."

"Don't get me wrong." Davis reached for the door. "They're talented and they have a lot of skills essential for today's market, some they may not even be aware of. It's just that a lot of them lack 'teachability', the kind of humility that shows they realize there's still more to learn. Growing up rarely hearing you're wrong or have made a mistake, not to mention that you've failed at something, can make for an unhealthy self-perception."

Jack nodded. "I don't know why mistakes and failures are so feared. It's when I do most of my growing and learning."

After saying his goodbyes and expressing his gratitude to Diane at the front desk, Davis led the way to the parking lot. "Sadly, coaching someone who lacks humility regardless of her experience level, is always difficult. When you do provide feedback, they're likely to be offended or caught off guard because they're not used to objective performance assessments."

"I don't understand. How do these people stick around? There are a few managers that seem to fit your description to a tee."

"Jack, they are talented enough to bring value to the organization, but it comes at a cost. Throughout their career they have projected an aura of, if you criticize me, I'll bite. They are porcupines. What happens is that people just avoid the difficult conversations and the porcupines remain frozen in their development often causing more damage than the value they bring. But that is for another conversation."

"I think you are right." Jack looked up and smiled. "And not for the first time today."

"Don't you know I'm always right?" Davis laughed. "The best way to avoid those situations is by hiring colleagues who want to be coached, people who already possess the qualities we're looking for."

Jack took out his keys. "You know, as we're talking, I'm thinking there's another great benefit to hiring people who are humble. They're more likely to ask for directions when they're lost or having trouble." He looked at Davis. "I can see where these qualities really pay off in more than one scenario."

Davis smiled. "Right, my friend. This is a journey for all of us and I'm most effective as a manager when my direct reports and teammates let me know what they need to be successful. People who are humble seek me out more often. And if you have a team that asks for directions or clarification when they're unsure about something, you have a more productive team."

"You mean the classic example of the guy who won't ask for directions and keeps driving around hoping he'll somehow find the way." Jack raised his hand. "Guilty—I admit it. And to add insult to injury, not only am I frustrated that I'm late, but I made it worse because I didn't ask for help initially which only compounded the problem."

Jack turned and walked toward his car. "Not asking for help in an organization kills productivity. And I need my team to know when they're lost and be able to admit it. It makes them nimbler, more responsive when issues arise."

"Correct." Davis agreed. "And issues happen with teams all the time. If on top of that they're bogged down because they can't admit there's a problem the timeframe for a response can be days or, worse, weeks. It's a horrifying thought, with a potentially devastating impact on performance and productivity. Nobody has that much time, especially in today's economy."

Jack nodded in agreement and turned towards his car. "Davis this was a great day. I've got lots to learn." He stopped and turn back towards his mentor. "Wait. I have another question."□

Discerning a Candidate's Humility

1. To assess humility, it's important to gauge how teachable a candidate is, meaning how receptive he or she is to feedback, correction, advice, and change. Here are some questions to help you assess this essential, need-to-hire characteristic:

    *   Have the candidate describe the last or the most challenging process she had to learn.
    *   Ask how she learns best, meaning through which methods, such as visual, mentoring, reading an evaluation, or other. Also, ask why this method works best.
    *   Ask the prospect for an example of a time she sought help or assistance and why. Ask what type of source she sought help from, for example, a colleague, the internet or from the help desk?
    *   Ask give me an example of the last time you were stumped and couldn't figure something out. What did you do to solve it?

2. To learn what type of environment a prospect learns best in:

    *   Who was your favorite professor or coach and why?
    *   Who was your best professor or coach and why?
    *   Who was your least favorite professor or coach and why?
    *   Who was your worst professor or coach and why?
    *   How did each of these professors and/or coaches try to motivate you? Which methods of motivation did you find most helpful and why?

3. Query the recruit about an important learning experience in his work or college experience:

    *   Ask why he chose and what he learned from that experience?

4. Ask the recruit to share a humbling moment or an experience where he was unprepared for the situation:

    *   Listen for how he describes the way he responded at the time of the incident.
    *   Listen for whether time and distance have given him a positive perspective.
    *   Ask whether the prospect has ever been criticized in front of others. Listen for how she reacted and how she describes the situation now. Tone tells a lot about attitude, and attitude says a lot about humility or the lack of it.

5. Look to discern not only whether the candidate prefers to work with others, on a team, or individually but also why.

    *   Those who nearly always prefer to work alone may be less likely to seek advice. If a prospect typically prefers to work alone, find out why. Regardless of how he likes to learn, pursue individuals who will seek guidance.

    *   Some employees who prefer solitary work may like to have a sense of control. If this is because they're self-starters and like taking the initiative, and if this approach matches the description of the open position, you may have the right person. However, some prospects feel they know best most of the time so working with others is just a chore and waste of their time.

6. Take note how seriously the candidate takes himself.

    *   Can the candidate laugh at his mistakes?
    *   Does the candidate use self-effacing humor?
    *   Is the candidate easily provoked when challenged or is she open to correction and feedback?

7. Without being obnoxious, look and listen for a detail, an error or something that could be obscure and challenge the candidate about its accuracy.

    *   How did the candidate respond? Was there gratitude for pointing out the error. Was there gratitude at the opportunity to clear the misunderstanding up?

    *   Did the candidate become flustered because he was being challenged or questioned?

8. Ask the candidate about a time when he made an incorrect choice.

    *   Ask how he corrected it and why he chose this approach.
    *   Ask what he learned from the experience.
    *   Ask how the candidate views those who give him advice or correction?

9. Query the candidate about her most satisfying win (for example, a competition, promotion, an award, grade, sale, or opportunity).

    *   Ask why she thinks she won? Was the effort all her own or does she recognize that others helped her get to the end?

    *   Ask if she interacted with the other contestants after receiving the award? What did that look like? Is she a gracious winner?

10. Query the candidate about his most difficult loss (for example, a competition, promotion, an award, grade, sale, or opportunity).
    - Ask what was most important about the loss, meaning what it represented to the candidate, such as years of effort.
    - Ask how he responded to the loss. Listen for answers like, "I did my best, but we just were outplayed." This answer and a reflective tone show that the respondent isn't looking to blame or point fingers.
    - Ask if he congratulated the winning party or team? Does the candidate seem to be a gracious loser?

11. Query the recruit about a time when a friend, coworker, or teammate let him down or betrayed him.
    - Ask if he sought to repair the relationship and why or why not. Also, ask what this looked and sounded like. Proud people have a hard time forgiving and are easily insulted. Look for the opposite in the hire.

12. Listen during the interview for whether the candidate talks incessantly and dominates the discussion with countless anecdotes.
    - This could be nerves, or it can signal a lack of humility. Try interrupting the prospect to see how she responds to interruption.

13. Ask about a time the candidate was in a debate over an issue and was wrong, or a time when he offended a fellow classmate, teammate, or colleague:
    - Ask if he admitted he was wrong; if so, ask how he did this.
    - Ask whether he made the situation right, to the best of his ability, with the other party involved.
    - Those who lack humility rarely see that they're wrong, and when they're wrong, they have a hard time admitting it and repairing damaged relationships.
    - Those who are humble are usually quicker to admit their mistakes and to seek to repair those relationships.

14. Does humility mean a person won't lead?
    - Absolutely not. Humility is a quality leaders must possess.
    - Leaders who believe they already know the answers and must be the smartest person in the room are ripe for eventual failure.
    - A humble leader values the input of his team and realizes that even

the newest member of the team can provide value.

Humble leaders can be the strongest and most inspiring kind of leader because they draw their people into the decision and problem-solving process.

15. Here are some key benefits of hiring humility:
   - Humble employees are willing and able to be taught new skills and to refine the skills they have.
   - They are life-long learners.
   - Modest employees tend to buy in sooner to the manager's and organization's plans and needs and those of the team.
   - When a modest individual is lost or needs direction, he seeks it more readily.
   - Humble colleagues tend to be better team players as they are open to giving and receiving correction and input.
   - They tend to treat others with respect because they don't see others as competition, but instead as valued teammates.

Defining Terms:
   - Humility: The ability and willingness to be taught or corrected and the desire to honor and lift others up before self.
   - In short: A teachable response.
   - Humbility: Humility and ability combined. A word that my daughter said by accident but captures the concept well.

CHAPTER 12
PUTTING THE PIECES TOGETHER

"The person who knows everything has a lot to learn."
-Author unknown

Davis waved him over, "What's your question?"

Jack walked quickly to Davis who had set his bag down as he looked for his key fob. "Can you take a look at something I've been mulling over?" Jack peered into his computer bag and pulled out a piece of paper. He set it down on the hood of Davis' car and made a rudimentary sketch and added a few notes. Jack looked at it and squinted. "Well, you'll get the idea," He held it out and waited for Davis to respond."

"Here they are," said Davis victoriously as he pocketed his key fob. Davis took the piece of paper and scanned the page.

"I'm a visual learner and I've had this image in my mind. Am I on the right track?" Jack asked cautiously. "It's a stool."

"Yes, I see the resemblance but—keep your day job, Jack." Davis rotated the page so he could read Jack's notes. "I like this. A four-legged stool and each leg labeled with the four qualities."

Jack smiled. "The seat is well supported, and each leg is important."

"This is good," said Davis approvingly. "Now take the first letter of each of the traits. What does it spell?"

Jack looked down. "W, I, M, H. WIMH—what does that mean?"

Davis grinned. "Try rearranging the letters, Webster."

Jack looked again. "WHIM—Hiring on a WHIM." He nodded. "I like it."

"Good," Davis affirmed. "Now if you remember the acronym, you'll remember the qualities to look for and hire. Believe me, if you don't use this approach, you'll never forget it—the hard way!"

Jack smiled. "I have to say, this whole process has been an education. I've appreciated your help and advice. The only thing is—" Jack's voice trailed off as he played with his keys.

"What is it? Be humble now—ask for directions." Davis smiled.

Jack smiled and shook his head. "Honestly. I'm a bit stress out thinking about this whole process—having to find and uncover all these qualities. You make it all look and sound simple but I'm barely keeping up."

Davis grinned. "The more you use the process the easier it gets—trust me on this. The hard part is knowing what you're looking for so that you'll recognize it when you see it." He pressed his key fob and started his car. "But I hear your frustration so let me caution you not to rush the process. It's better to leave a position vacant a little longer than fill it with someone who lacks these qualities. If you hire in haste, you'll regret it in leisure and with a full, but dysfunctional team. And guess who has to clean up the mess in aisle seven."

"Me. I've dealt with enough messes. I'm so ready to put my mop and bucket away." Jack pointed to the picture. "If you had to pick just one WHIM quality, which stands out most in your mind?"

Davis glanced down at Jack's sketch. "Good question but a hard one. You said that each leg is important. Jack each leg is essential." He tapped on the paper for emphasis. "If possible, you need to hire all four. Think back to the hires that didn't work out or those difficult colleagues that you struggle with. I'll bet they are missing or weak in one of these areas. Hiring a candidate who is missing one or two will eventually come to haunt you and your organization."

"I believe that. It is easy to see how things can go south when one or two of these qualities is missing. I guess I was just wondering if one stood out to you as more important?"

Davis paused. "Have you noticed how beautifully the qualities of WHIM overlap? Maturity and humility are a good example. We must be teachable and hungry for personal growth. That is why I love humility so much. Humility enables us to learn from life's lessons which leads to Maturity which then brings stability. I need to have emotionally stable people who are willing to learn. Humility and maturity are a powerful combination which also feed and support Work Ethic and integrity.

"Yes, I see that. It makes sense. So, what is your go-to question for this power pair?"

"You heard it today—several times. I want to hear about a difficult event or a major obstacle in his life, at least one that was key for him. And I listen as he discusses the experience and what it taught him. How he grew from it. Specifically, I listen for whether he looks back on it with bitterness as an excuse for life's shortcomings or can he look back and see blessings that came out of it. A rich time of growth and learning."

"I think I'm getting the hang of this." Jack paused. "I've always been so focused on a candidate's skills that I didn't pay much attention to—WHIM. Where do skills and training fit into the equation?"

"These are great questions, Jack." Davis checked his watch. "Let me give you a quick overview. First if we are hiring an accountant or pilot then, of course, we need to interview accountants and pilots and of those make sure that the one we choose has WHIM. But there are many jobs in which the skills can be taught. Say for example a sales position. Someone may not have much or any sales experience but if they have WHIM, I know they will work hard, strive, are teachable, coachable, accountable and honest. I'll take a candidate like that any day."

Jack nodded in agreement. "Fortunately, most of the candidates we are meeting are not a blank slate like that but understand the position and think they already have skills and experiences that will add value. Then it's our job to improve upon those foundations."

Davis leaned on his opened car door. In my mind, there are two big boxes I'm trying to place a checkmark in with each new hire. Do they have WHIM and is the job they are applying for a fit? Remember Jack, a lot of the recruits we see on campus and the recent grads we see off-campus aren't sure what they want to do—they're still finding themselves, learning their likes and dislikes. Some organizations won't look at candidates who don't have two to five years of experience in the workforce. Remember Nate?"

Jack smiled. "Barely."

"Do you recall what he said he wanted to do for a living?"

"He said he didn't know for sure, but he thought he'd like to try what we're doing. And that was based on a friend in a similar position who he thinks likes his job."

"Exactly. And he wanted to try the job out on our time and our dime. What he's really saying is that he wants to try on a few careers, like buying a new pair of sneakers. We're looking for candidates who already have an understanding of their skills and talents. That way, when we find and hire them we serve both their best interests and ours. And that includes our colleagues and the other employees."

"Funny you should mention that, "Jack said. "I graduated with people who've changed jobs and whole careers two or three times already. I was complaining to Carol that the Bureau of Labor Statistics states that between the ages of eighteen to twenty-four the average worker held five and a half jobs in six years. That was the big reason I gave her as to why I thought my new hires were leaving."

"Yes, youth can be a factor but regardless of age, I find retention increases when I hire WHIM and fit. Fit meaning do they have the skills or transferable skills and do their interests fit the job they are applying for?

"Exactly." Davis climbed into his car. "Hey, listen, I've enjoyed interviewing with you. Your instincts and insights into the candidates and your energy are a pleasure. Let's finish the process here next week on Wednesday. We'll meet Sharon for breakfast at eight in the student union and then have our follow-up with Brett over lunch. I'll call them both to confirm."

"Sounds like a plan," Jack affirmed. "I'm pumped about both of them."

Davis opened the car window. "I almost forgot. I'll send you some links to articles on coaching and working with college grads. The information will help you understand the candidates better. Once you take a look, formulate some questions and scenarios aimed at triggering a response. You can ask about poor reviews, disappointing grades, long work weeks, projects that took more time than expected, that kind of thing."

"Great, that should yield some interesting responses." Jack tucked his tablet under his arm. "Oh, I kept meaning to ask—why were you so upfront with Sharon and Brett about wanting to pursue them? I never tip my hand. I want them to pursue us. That's how I know they want the job and to work with Omega."

Davis smiled. "I used to feel the same. But when you find a great candidate you need to do the pursuing because the candidates you think are excellent will be seen as such by other companies. That's why it's best to move through the process efficiently and develop the relationship at the same time. If you don't, you can lose the person to another company that works faster."

"I guess that makes sense. Regardless of the job market, good talent is always a premium."

Davis tapped on his steering wheel. "Oh, just to be clear, I'm only direct with candidates who I think have great potential. There is one other advantage to developing a more personal relationship with candidates. What do you think candidates are looking for in a company or manager?"

"Good money, opportunity, and a healthy environment to work in?"

"Those are all important Jack, but candidates are looking for WHIM as well. Think about the managers you've worked with and for. Does WHIM matter? What about the company's goals and values? Don't you want to see an organization that reflects your character and values?"

Jack fumbled with his keys as he nodded in agreement. "That makes perfect sense. They are interviewing us as well."

"Very well. It's been a great day. Next week at the student union then." Jack waved and went over to his car. Finally, he thought, things were looking up, and they were nearing the finish line. At least he hoped they were.□

The Candidate Hiring Checklist

1. Here are ways you can make sure you have a candidate with all four WHIM qualities:
    *   Note each quality of WHIM and leave space for notes.
    *   Next to each quality note which activities, experiences, and outcomes apply. Remember that there is overlap, so one observation might apply to more than one quality. For example, receiving a poor yearly review may have sparked a commitment to seeking out a mentor which improved his outcomes. Where would you place this?
        o   Work Ethic: He was committed to improving his outcomes and did so based on reviews and assessments.
        o   Humility: Hearing he needed to improve, listening to feedback and then seeking out a solution.
        o   Maturity: He chose to not be offended or bitter and instead chose to be better.
    *   There will be times when an interview ends and during your assessment, you will notice that one quality is not as strong or apparent as the others.
        o   This may be because time ran out or that you unknowingly zeroed in on other qualities. Make a commitment during the second interview to uncover evidence for this quality
        o   There will also be times where one quality just doesn't seem as strong as the others. That is ok, but it must be identifiable and present before you hire.

2. Make sure to ask questions that require your prospects to give examples of each WHIM quality:
    *   Use the STAR method. Specific questions should produce specific answers:
    *   At the beginning of each interview explain to the candidate that you would like the candidate to answer questions using a STAR response.
        o   ST: Situation or Task. Make sure that the response is about a specific event rather than, "Most of the times when I'm in that situation I...."
        o   Action: What specific action did the candidate take
        o   Result: What was the specific result.

3. Take time to review your candidates with a respected colleague:

- In this example, Jack was required by his supervisor to work with Davis. If you're hiring on your own, have a colleague quiz you about how well the candidate exhibited each of the WHIM qualities. Encourage the colleague to push you.
    - o It is easy to get caught up in the excitement of meeting a quality candidate. Having someone else challenge your assessments about each quality is an import component of making sure we make better decisions and is a good sign of a manager's humility and maturity. It is not about being proven right or wrong but about making an excellent decision.
    - o Remember the example of Steve? Davis became focused on one quality. Having a colleague quiz you about your decision may help uncover a flaw in your thinking.
    - o Be humble throughout the process. Keeping emotionally distant and transparent about your assessments will pay off because you may pick up on something that was not initially apparent.
        - ▪ For example, you may have not received a STAR answer to work ethic but just their word that they usually out-perform their peers. The candidate may be accurate, but I'd like to see the data behind their self-assessment.
            - • The danger in this scenario is that if you want this candidate to move through the process then you may be more likely to accept a non-STAR answer.

4. What are your instincts and insights about the candidate?
    - Do you have an initial positive/negative biases that you need to challenge? "She's a soccer player. I'm a soccer player. She is like me and must be great." "Five years at a Community College. Must not have been able to get into a good college because of his grades which is why it took him five years." Of course, both of these are foolish and without merit but if left unchecked they might sit just below the surface of our thinking.
    - What is your gut telling you? Do you like this candidate? Do you see them fitting into your organization?
    - Be aware of becoming overly enamored with one or two WHIM qualities. One or two outstanding qualities may eclipse a gap in another quality. If this happens, you'll regret it, and so will your organization and colleagues.

5. Consider whether the candidate, though perhaps lacking one or more of the four WHIM qualities, still has room for growth

- If you notice a candidate lacks or is weak in a certain WHIM quality, ask yourself whether he has potential and whether you can work with him to develop what he may be missing.
    o If you believe the four WHIM qualities are non-negotiable and non-teachable, why take the risk since it is very difficult if not impossible to develop these qualities in a manager-employee relationship.
- Instead of hiring the candidate, encourage her to seek out experiences and opportunities that will expose her to grow in these areas. For example, if someone's work ethic is a concern, she might want to gain sales experience and demonstrate her ability to drive sales and to seek growth opportunities beyond her stated job requirements.

CHAPTER 13
SHARON

"As a face is reflected in water, so the heart reflects the person."
Proverbs 27:19

The next week Jack pulled up beside Davis in the parking lot behind the Susque State College student union. Davis gathered his cell, tablet, and file and stepped out of the car.

"How long have you been here?" Jack shouted as he made his way towards the bench on which Davis sat.

"About twenty minutes." Davis stood and smiled. "Ready to find the right candidate?"

"That's the goal. Hey, I heard one of your employees was promoted to manager last week," Jack said as they walked into the student union. "Congratulations."

"Thanks. Holly's terrific. I'm very proud of her."

"I remember when she first started with the company. Did you hire her?"

"Sure did." Davis grinned. "She's another great example of someone who possessed all traits we're looking for and wound up doing a great job."

"So, I heard." Jack paused. "I know she was a star athlete, hard worker and all but with everything we've been talking about, I was wondering if maybe she was just one of those people who lived a charmed life yet lacked maturity because she didn't face much in the way of obstacles."

Davis led the way into the Union's narthex. "What makes you say that?"

"Well, she's one of those people who just seems to have it all. She's personable, fit, went to a great school and landed a great job and has been extremely successful. Seems to me she got sprinkled with fairy dust. Did she have maturity when you hired her?"

Davis nodded. "That's what makes Holly so great—you wouldn't know just by talking with her or working with her the difficulties she went through early on. She lost her mom when she was a kid. A few years later she lost a sibling."

"What?" Jack stopped in the hallway. "Wow. I never knew that."

"It's not a secret—she just doesn't talk about it much," Davis said. "Not as a first topic of conversation anyway. And you don't hear any bitterness in her voice when she does talk about it. She's an example of someone who used her difficult experiences as launch pads."

"I guess so. She's one of the most positive people I know," Jack agreed. "I'd love to find a Holly today."

They walked into the dining hall and found Sharon waiting, ten minutes early. Jack and Davis looked at each other.

"Well, she's on time," Jack said with a grin.

The three got breakfast in the student union café and went to sit down. At first, Sharon struggled a bit to get comfortable and looked unsure of whether to eat, take notes, or just talk. She soon settled on all three.

Davis began asking questions, starting with the familiar. "So, Sharon, take me back through your time from when you were a senior in high school up to today."

Jack looked down at his tray. Why was Davis asking the same opening question, he wondered. He glanced at Sharon. She looked puzzled but only for a moment. Then she began retelling her history. A few minutes in, Davis asked about the leadership role she had taken on her swim and track teams.

"So, tell me about your toughest wins and losses," Davis asked.

Sharon described examples of both then transitioned to her college years. Davis persisted with some of the same queries about the difficult situations she had been through during that time. In each response, Sharon handled herself gracefully, with confidence and poise, and with the same enthusiasm. Jack found himself interested in the stories as if hearing them for the first time.

Davis paused. "You mentioned the lacrosse tournament in Bermuda and that a few of the starters on the team broke curfew. What happened with that?"

"A couple of our best players went out drinking, clearly breaking the policies of our team and the school. I found out about the incident and as team captain had to make the tough call to sit them out of the final game."

"That must have been difficult," Jack said quietly.

Sharon looked at Jack, "It was, I have to admit. But those players let the whole team down, not just me, and they knew it. Having to sit out a championship game gave them a chance to think about that." Sharon smiled. "But everything worked out okay in the end. We went on to win and that was satisfying. Even if we didn't win and it was due to our starters sitting out, it was the right decision."

Recalling Davis's advice to ask a question to generate an emotional response, Jack asked Sharon to describe a situation where she was criticized for her work and how she had handled it.

Sharon paused a moment, collecting her thoughts. "Last summer during my internship I worked for CoTria, a consulting company in New Jersey. I oversaw logistics. Some of the more important items on my list of responsibilities were making travel arrangements and ensuring the meeting rooms set and ready for each seminar. I enjoyed the position and I'll have to admit, I did a great job—until Boston."

Jack interrupted, "I feel like some dire music should be playing at this point."

Sharon smiled, "That would be appropriate. The company policy is for the meeting rooms to be set up the night before the session. That means the meeting room arranged, the technology tested, and all the materials set out. My plane was late getting into Boston so when I arrived at the hotel, I was exhausted. I decided I'd get to bed as soon as possible and then get up early to set up."

"Sounds reasonable. And—I'll bet the technology didn't work. Am I right?"

"Nope. We had a great meeting. It went off without a hitch and my boss, Gerry, received rave reviews. I collected the feedback forms and brought them up to the front and congratulated him on a great presentation. His response was tempered, to say the least. I sensed something was bothering him and then I heard the dreaded, 'can I talk with you?'"

"Yikes," said Jack.

"He asked me if I knew what time the room was supposed to be set up? I said, Yes, but I told him that I was exhausted and that I decided to get up early, leaving me plenty of time to set up and I didn't think that would be a problem."

Davis nodded as he followed along. "Go on."

"Gerry stood up and stepped closer to me and said he had checked in to the hotel about an hour after I did and had stopped in to check on the room. He asked me if I knew why the procedure existed? I confessed I didn't. He said, 'Because experience has taught us that it is not sufficient to begin setting up the morning of the program. Too many things can go wrong. For example, what happens if the technology doesn't work and the IT guy is stuck in traffic. What happens if the wrong workshop materials were sent and you must order a last-minute print job? What happens if the room has been configured incorrectly and the meeting planner doesn't get in until later that morning?' He was very frustrated with me."

"Okay, I get it. But everything ran great. Did it seem like Gerry was nitpicking?"

"Of course, that was my first reaction but then I began to think about each of the scenarios he painted and then a bunch of others he didn't. I realized he was right. If problems are identified the night before, then I have more time to plan and make adjustments. I was wrong because I assumed that everything would fall into line, help would be available, the venue would be responsive and flexible, the materials were correct, and the technology would all work as expected. Thinking about what could have gone wrong, literally makes my heart race." Sharon looked down and took a breath. "Am I sweating?"

Davis shook his head no and smiled empathetically. "How did you respond to his strong feedback?"

"It stung. It took me off guard—especially after such a great program that ran flawlessly. And then I thought. What would happen if it didn't run flawlessly? What might have happened if the equipment didn't work, or the room wasn't ready to be occupied, or the materials were wrong? My boss's livelihood and his company's reputation depend on great outcomes and he can't have those outcomes if we have problems, especially preventable problems that could—."

Both Davis and Jack distracted Sharon as they simultaneously made a few notations. Davis looked up and smiled, "Sorry it's a bad habit of mine. I tend to jot notes down while you are talking so I don't forget the details. Please continue."

"—I realized he was right, and I was wrong. What I thought was no big deal was actually very important. Those procedures were established because of hard lessons learned. When he finished addressing me, I felt like someone had punched me in the gut. I gathered my thoughts and apologized. I said that I was aware of the procedures but thought I'd be fine if I waited until morning. I was wrong for doing so. I asked for his forgiveness and told him it would never happen again. And it never did happen again because he fired me."

"What? That's awful," said Jack.

Sharon smiled widely and laughed. "No, I'm just kidding. He accepted my apology and I learned a valuable lesson. There are reasons behind rules and precedents and if I'm ever unsure, I should seek to understand why these procedures are in place and if need be, ask for permission if I feel there needs to be a change or exception."

"Well done Sharon. Well done." Davis returned to Sharon's timeline and continued to probe for areas of concern and confirmation of his conclusions from last week's interview.

An hour and a half later, the interview ended and nearly as quickly as it had begun, Jack thought. All in all, it was a positive exchange, including Sharon's insightful follow-up questions, which Jack noticed were different from what she asked during the first interview. She had clearly taken the advice to read through the Omega materials on first career choices and had paid attention.

Davis checked his cell. "Well, Sharon, it was a pleasure talking with you. I'll get back to you in the next day or two."

"Thanks," Sharon said. "I enjoyed speaking with you both." She stood, shook hands, and maintained eye contact. "I like the sound of this opportunity and just want to say again that I feel it matches my abilities and what I'm looking for." She smiled and picked up her folder.

Once Sharon left, Jack checked his tablet and made a note. "Wow, time sure flew by with that interview." He got up and grabbed his mug. "I'm going to cap this off. I figure you want tea, right?"

Davis grinned. "Please."

Jack returned with two steaming cups and sat down. "I have a question—we already knew Sharon's history so why the same questions?"

Davis put down his cup. "I like to ask a few of the same questions again to see if the stories are consistent and to fill any holes I notice after the first interview, especially if they're in the timeline. Listening for consistent responses also serves as an integrity check. It reinforces that the candidate isn't trying to hide something. Once I'm satisfied that's not the case, I pick a few areas to probe."

"Makes sense." Jack grinned. "I think I'll steal that idea."

Davis looked over his notes. "So, what do you think? Did any questions or answers stand out during Sharon's interview?"

"Yes. When you asked about Bermuda, she gave an honest answer and I liked her reasoning—a lot." He paused. "It made me wonder if I could have done the same."

Davis smiled. "I'm way too competitive to take a loss on account of missing a curfew." He grinned. "I'm joking. I thought Sharon made the right choice."

"She even went on to score three times to assure a victory. I like that kind of fire." Jack tipped back his chair. "So, considering what we know are our must-haves, where would you say Sharon stands?"

"Well, she's got work ethic—team captain, four years varsity field hockey—and good grades. She's got that covered."

"I agree," Jack affirmed. He extended his second finger, then stopped, furrowed his brow, and glanced at his notes. "Humility ..." His voice trailed off. "I have to say I still have a hard time recognizing that one. What stood out for you during her interviews that would show humility?"

"Well, the way she responded to tough questions, for one. For example, when I probed about the decisions she made and why she made them she wasn't defensive. She didn't get irritated that someone was questioning her reasoning."

"True," Jack affirmed. "She even seemed enthusiastic about sharing her rationale and without an air of superiority."

"Exactly. I often pursue questions just beyond a candidate's comfort zone to see how the person reacts. I did that especially with Sharon's leadership decisions and she did great in how she answered. And did you notice that when she was in line getting her food, she asked the server about her birthday?"

"I did notice," Jack said. "Now that you mention it, I also heard her congratulate the security guard on his alma mater's big win last weekend. She clearly takes a genuine interest in other people. I guess it's a mark of humility to look for opportunities to acknowledge others, honor their interests."

"That's right," Davis acknowledged. "And she took notes during both interviews, which shows she's engaged and organized. Not only that but did you notice that this time around she anticipated I'd be here and brought along an extra copy of her resume and timeline?

"True. I also liked that she came with questions that clearly showed she read the Omega material you gave her last week. She obviously took the advice you gave her last week and read through the packet."

He paused. Jack held up a third finger. "Okay, so Sharon has work ethic, humility, and next is integrity. I don't know how many too many competitive athletes who would make the kind of leadership decision Sharon did about her team's curfew and stand by it. If she can do the right thing when a game is on the line, I don't think I'd have trouble trusting her in a job situation." Jack looked wistful. "It would be great to not have to look over an employee's shoulder every minute to make sure she's doing the work."

"Exactly," Davis agreed. "So, what does that leave us with?"

Jack held his fourth finger up and smiled. "Maturity—I think Sharon's entire interview spoke to that. She's been through a lot in life and the hardships seem to have shaped her character in a positive way. I didn't sense a bitter attitude."

"Great," Davis affirmed. "That means she passes the WHIM test. Now let me ask you this. What does your instinct tell you?"

Jack smiled. "Now I see why you ask that question last. Considering all Sharon's qualities as they came through in these two interviews, I have a good feeling about her and her attitude. I can see myself and the team working with her and I think she would respond well to coaching. All in all, my instincts say she's a great candidate and would be a quality hire."

Davis nodded. "I feel the same. And that's after taking inventory of any preconceived ideas or prejudices, making sure all four WHIM qualities are present and checking my instincts. After doing all that, I'd still say Sharon is a great candidate."

Jack smiled. "Okay, but remember, we're hiring for my opening."

"Agreed," Davis said with a grin. "But that's another perk of interviewing a great candidate—it's encouraging to everybody."

Jack tucked Sharon's resume into his folder. "One other question—why are we interviewing in the cafeteria? I thought the interview rooms at Career Services were a lot more professional."

"I wondered if you might say something. After the first interview, I like seeing candidates in other settings. It broadens the scope of the experience, more like actually being on the job. And it provides an opportunity for the unexpected. For example, if we hadn't all grabbed a bite to eat or stood in line, we wouldn't have had a chance to see Sharon interact with the woman behind the counter or the security guard. Impromptu moments like those reveal the candidate's true personality. You wouldn't see that in a regular sit-down interview."

"Makes sense," Jack agreed. "Most candidates can put on a good face in a controlled environment. We want to see them as real as possible."

"Exactly," Davis affirmed. "Now let's take a look at the next file."

Davis and Jack spent the next fifteen minutes reviewing their notes and getting ready to see Brett, who walked into the student union ten minutes early.

Jack nudged Davis. "I knew I liked this guy." ☐ ☐

The Second Interview: Mix It Up

A second interview, especially one in a different setting, offers a chance to see the real candidate behind the resume. Here are tips on making the most of the time and opportunity.

1. Meet candidates in a new setting to see different sides of their personalities:
   - For consistency, keep the first interview more formal and consistent. Introduce the new setting once you moved into the second or third interview.
   - Watch for how the candidate reacts to other people, especially those who serve them, for example:
     o In a self-service environment, notice whether the candidate cleans up after himself or leaves it for someone else to.
     o Does the recruit look to be helpful to others, for example, helping clear everyone's tray, offering to help carry purchased items, holding the door for others, inviting others to order first? Is she servant-minded, or is she looking to be served?
     o In a public setting, watch for whether the candidate seeks opportunities to engage with others.
   - A different setting can create tension which can illuminate how the candidate responds in new or stressful situations.

2. If you have doubts about a certain quality, review his timeline and look for opportunities to probe the area in question until you are fully satisfied:
   - Be specific in your questions and be redundant; you want to see how the candidate reacts in those instances, for example, whether she is uncomfortable or easily frustrated by questions about her line of reasoning and how she handles those moments.

3. If you gave a recruit feedback or advice during the first interview, check to see whether he listened and acted on the advice or suggestion:
   - For example, if you gave the prospect an information packet, ask questions to see if he read it and how closely he paid attention to the content.
   - Ask if the recruit had done any additional research on the position, company, or industry. Doing so would indicate a recruit's effort to make sure that this position, company, and industry were a fit for

her.

- Ask if the recruit attempted to reach out to anyone who had worked at the company or industry.
- Ask if the recruit had checked to see if she was LinkedIn with anyone

in the company or industry. This type of preparation shows initiative, curiosity and attention to detail.

4. If your instinct is telling you something isn't right, now is the time to listen!

- If you are uncertain about a candidate, it is better to wait and address the concerns than to assume, overlook a red flag, or neglect your instincts. If you hire in haste, you'll regret it over time.

CHAPTER 14
BRETT

"As a face is reflected in water, so the heart reflects the person."
Proverbs 27:19

Jack waved as he and Davis approached Brett, who had arrived early. "Good to see you," Jack said and gestured toward The Grill.

Brett greeted both interviewers with a strong handshake and a smile then handed each a copy of a news article titled, "Red Sox, Set to Repeat."

Davis smiled but looked surprised. "What's this?"

Brett grinned. "Last time we met, Jack and I were talking about the Red Sox's amazing sweep through the playoffs. He mentioned that you're both fans so I thought you might like to see this. It kills me to fuel your pride, since your team beat mine in the playoffs, but the Sox did have an amazing run."

They all laughed, but Davis made a mental note of Brett's ability to listen and follow up.

Once seated, Davis asked Brett to review his last year. Satisfied with the consistency of Brett's answers, Davis focused on his work ethic. "How would you compare your productivity to that of other people you've worked with?"

Brett tapped his resume. "Hine Brothers Homes is a premier home builder in this area, and I had a great opportunity to do an internship with them as a project manager."

"Project manager—sounds like a great opportunity," Jack put in. Somehow, he doubted Brett's father had gotten him the job, but this time around he wanted to be sure. "What were your responsibilities?"

"Once the homes were sold, I made sure the customers were happy with the way the homes were being constructed. I earned the nickname 'Shoeless' because I always took my shoes off during our morning team meetings."

Davis and Jack simultaneously peeked under the table.

"Yes, I have my shoes on." Brett said with a laugh.

Davis smiled. "Well, inquiring minds want to know—how did you earn such a reputation?"

"As you might imagine," Brett continued, "a lot of homeowners tend to micromanage the construction of their homes and at times can be quite demanding. I'd get calls at all hours about the issues that irked them." He sighed. "Some issues were pretty farfetched, but the clients were paying a lot of money for their homes and my job was to make sure they had a great building experience."

"Good approach," Jack agreed. "I've been in my house eight years and I still have a dozen items that were never taken care of. It left a bad impression on my wife and me."

"Sorry you had that experience," Brett said. "I didn't want any of my customers saying that about my—I mean, their—homes. Most mornings I'd be on the job site at six, investigating and fixing the easier problems myself. By the time we had our team meeting at eight, I'd take off my mud-caked shoes before I went into the building."

Jack grinned. "What did your boss say about that?"

"During my final review, he asked if I thought it was strange that I always came to meetings dirty and without any shoes." Brett sat back in his chair. "I told him I never wondered why I was dirty. I just wondered why everyone else was clean."

Jack laughed. "Excellent—a classic line if I ever heard one."

As Brett's interview continued on a positive track, Jack found it easier and easier to see himself working with him.

"All right, let's turn to your grades for a few minutes." Davis looked over Brett's transcript and saw the D in organic chemistry. "Tell me about organic chemistry."

The table fell silent. Jack shot Davis a look, but Davis kept his eyes on Brett. Why in the world was Davis beating up this great recruit over one grade, Jack wondered. Brett is clearly an outstanding candidate, and Jack found himself hoping Davis wouldn't blow this opportunity.

Brett fidgeted. "To be honest, it was a subject I didn't enjoy, and every class was an effort to get through. I did a poor job on my term project, which accounted for over fifty percent of the grade, and I suffered for it. I also made some bad decisions along the way." He looked at both Davis and Jack. "But I take full responsibility for the grade."

Brett pointed to the transcript. "Besides the D in that class, the lowest grades I got all throughout college were two C pluses."

"I noticed," Davis said with a smile. "I thought there might be more to the story."

"Isn't that the semester you had one of your surgeries?" Jack interjected.

"Yes, but that surgery was minor compared to the rest," Brett noted. "I still could've done a better job in the course. I just dropped the ball."

For the next forty minutes, Davis and Jack had a lively back and forth with Brett. Probing areas of concern and then spending time evaluating Brett's fit with the company and team.

Satisfied with what he heard; Davis nodded. "So, do you have any questions for us?"

Brett tapped his tablet. "Actually, I do have a few. Davis, during our first interview you mentioned this job can breed mediocrity—what did you mean by that?"

Davis grinned. He appreciated when candidates took notes. He wasn't always sure what they were writing, but taking notes made them look engaged and at least showed that they thought enough of what he was saying to write it down.

"First, let me compliment you on taking and referring to your notes," Davis affirmed. "Sometimes people jot down names and numbers and other details on scraps of paper or somewhere in their phones and can't find them. It looks like you've developed some good habits."

Davis answered Brett's question and two others then drew the interview to a close. "One last thing—I'd like you to write a one-page paper by next Monday on qualities you think are most important for success in this industry."

Brett grinned. "Guess it's never too late in life for homework." He wrote down the assignment then stood and shook hands, looking both interviewers in the eye and expressing his enthusiasm at the prospect of joining their team. "If you choose to offer me the position you won't regret hiring me."

Jack watched as Brett left. "Would you tell a guy that big he can't have the job?" He laughed. "I have to say, that was a great interview."

"It was," Davis agreed. "Now it's time to review the WHIM list."

Jack nodded. "I was pretty sure Brett had a solid work ethic based on the first interview but your probing more in the second confirmed it."

"I knew he liked sports and held a few jobs, but I wanted a concrete picture of whether work ethic is part of his character," Davis noted. "His example of showing up muddy was an excellent insight into his thinking. It's an out-of-the-box approach, which is refreshing when it makes sense, which in this case it did. And he was comfortable with being different if it worked toward the goal of his customers having a great experience."

"Agreed," Jack affirmed. "That brings us to the next on the list—humility. I didn't see anything that put me off today. I just got the sense that Brett is someone who wants to learn and get better. A teachable spirit."

"Teachable spirit," Davis repeated. "That's the phrase to remember. Oh, and I forgot to mention when I left Brett a voicemail on his cell about our first interview his greeting was him and a friend rapping some bazar message. I left the voicemail, but suggested Brett evaluate his- greeting now that he's job hunting. When I called for this second interview, I heard a very simple and professional introduction. He listened and learned—that's teachable!"

Jack paused. "I would hope he'd listen. It's good advice."

Davis shook his head. "You'd be surprised how many candidates dress inappropriately and say it's just the way they express themselves or that the outrageous ring tone is personal and not business. Or they tell me the way they behave is part of their 'style.'"

"Since that isn't true with Brett, we're on to integrity," Jack said. "I thought he had that one after the first interview so that means we're on to—"

"Easy there Speed Racer!" Davis held up his hand. "Before you leave integrity let me tell you what I heard when I asked Brett about his grades."

"Now that you mention it, I did think the question seemed like kind of a cheap shot," Jack observed. "Especially after all Brett went through."

"There's a method to my madness," Davis said with a smile. "Brett could have leaned on one of at least five legitimate excuses as to why he didn't get a better grade but what was his answer?"

"He took full responsibility for the low grade even after I offered him an out and admitted he dropped the ball." Jack nodded. "I really like this guy."

"So, do I. But I like to ask about a candidate's worst grade or a difficult year-end review and the circumstances surrounding it. Oftentimes I hear it was because of a terrible teacher or boss, or that everyone did poorly in the class. Either that or the teacher or boss had something against the person, or the subject wasn't relevant to the person's major. Those are excuses, not reasons, and we don't have room for excuses."

"Agreed." Jack asserted. "The last thing I want now is an employee who won't take responsibility and admit when he fails to execute."

"Exactly. You can teach people who admit their mistakes, but you can't teach or help people develop who make excuses for their performance. So, I give Brett high marks on integrity."

"So, then, maturity." Jack felt energized. "Brett's answers about the poor grade, the struggles he went through and his outlook on life and work are excellent. I'd pass him with flying colors!"

"So, would I," Davis affirmed.

Jack put down his tablet. "That means we have two candidates who both did a great job. Now the problem is, how do I decide which to hire?"

"Listen, you have an opening, I have an opening. We're both walking out of here with a terrific new hire. Can you call each of their references?"

"Absolutely," Jack agreed.

"Then the next step is for you to sit down and list each member of your current team," Davis said. "Then list all the skills and assets each person brings to the table. Once you've done that ask yourself which of these two great candidates would best fit and augment your team. Once you compare their skills and abilities with your team's needs, you'll have your answer."

Jack grinned. "Sounds reasonable—and like we said, a baseball coach doesn't need five third-basemen."

Davis picked up his tablet and cell. "Exactly. Listen, let's stop by Career Services on our way out and thank them for their hard work."

Diane Raines saw them come through the door from her desk and greeted Davis with a smile. "So how did Brett and Sharon do?"

Davis sighed. "Complete train wrecks, as usual."

"Oh, stop." Diane turned to Jack. "Don't listen to him. We always give him our best."

Davis laughed. "Actually, Jack and I liked them both. And if everything checks out, we'll probably make offers to each—but don't mention anything until we decide who goes where."

"Of course," Diane nodded. "I'm so excited for them." The phone rang, and she glanced at the display. "Sorry, guys, duty calls. Great seeing you both and congratulations."

Davis and Jack walked out to the parking lot. Jack started toward his car then stopped. "You know, I think I owe you an apology."

Davis paused. "An apology?"

"When we first spoke a couple of weeks ago, I had a pretty bad attitude. I wanted to work together on the hiring process about as much as I wanted a root canal. I wasn't displaying one of the key elements we look for in everyone else—humility—I didn't want to admit that my process was broken and that there might be a better way."

Davis chuckled. "Having reservations, initially resisting change, those don't signal a lack of humility. I could tell you were forced into meeting with me, but you quickly got on board and you've demonstrated an ability and willingness to learn. I think you're a great example of humility. And I'm glad I could provide a few insights into my hiring practices."

"One of the things I've learned is that I don't know everything I need to about hiring," Jack observed. "Which is why I kept making the same mistakes over and over and getting the same results. You've shown me that hiring is easy. Well—not easy but simple. It's like I've always known these elements were important and valuable, but I never had a tool or framework to guide me. This has been great."

Davis grinned. "I arrived at WHIM after years of getting it wrong. I'm glad I could spare you some of the pain I endured. Spend this weekend thinking about your team and their skills and assets. Then ask yourself which candidate would best augment the team."

"Let's sit on this over the weekend and talk on Monday. Then I'll let you in on one last tip."

A Better Second Interview

The second and subsequent interviews are the time to double-check what you've learned about your prospect and plug any information gaps. These concepts will help with that process.

1. During any additional interviews, ask a few of the same or similar questions as in the first interview:
    *   Asking questions that cover old ground will ensure consistency.
    *   Other questions about how a candidate got the job or experience, advanced, performed or ended their tenure might be of interest.

2. While a candidate is talking about a past job, listen for the names of managers or bosses then ask:
    *   Would you mind if I call this person?
        o   Does the candidate seem open maybe even excited for you to call?
    *   If I call him or her, what would this person say about your work ethic, humility, integrity, and maturity?
    *   Always follow through with reference checks.

3. Does the candidate have well-thought-out questions, or is she "winging" it?
    *   Do the questions reveal that the candidate has done some research or looked more closely at the industry?
    *   When I would ask candidates how they prepared for the interview, it always bothered me when they would say I glanced at your website.
        o   Did they look at the organization's core values? Do they know the mission statement? Do they know any history? What was the last product the organization introduced? Has the organization been in the news lately?
        o   The second interview is not just about the interviewer learning more it is also about the candidate digging deeper and learning more about the organization. Is there evidence that he has done so?

4. Do you have areas of concern? While being courteous and polite, ask the hard or uncomfortable questions.
    *   Questions like, why did your tenure end with that volunteer organization? Why do you think your sales suffered in your third year? I see it took you five years to complete your degree, was that

part of your plan?

- These types of questions are not intended to be 'gotcha' questions. These are intended to shed light in areas of question. You may hear back, "Yes, it did take me five years instead of four but that was because I worked full-time and had to pay for college myself." Wow, that is a wonderful insight into who this candidate is. Again, never a gotcha style questions.

5. Between the first and second interviews:
   - Has the candidate learned more about the organization?
     - o Similar to question 3. What sources did he use? Does this show a general curiosity about this career path? Did he do anything out of the ordinary to track down sources or additional information?
   - Did he reach out to any past or current employees to get a candid assessment of the position and career path he is interviewing for?
   - Did he learn anything about the organization that has positively or negatively affected his opinion of the organization?

6. Give the candidate a piece of advice during the interview, and see whether and how well she heeds it:
   - Examples include voicemail introductions, the appropriate attire for your particular workplace, a book to read, blog or website to review, watching an informative video, bringing multiple resumes in case there is more than one interviewer, and pointing out an aspect of the resume they might adjust or fix.

7. Give the candidate a brief assignment:
   - How does she react when you assigned her the task?
   - Does she complete the task on time, or early?
   - Did she complete the assignment correctly and does she follow directions?
   - If not, what were her excuses?
   - Is she able to communicate or interpret data appropriately?
   - Did she take pride in her work?

8. Be careful not to become overly enamored with certain aspects of a candidate's character:
   - Try and remain unbiased and open throughout the process. Remember how Davis's starry-eyed view of Steve's work ethic caused Davis to look past Steve's other, less desirable traits. A

strong trait cannot compensate for a weak or missing trait.

CHAPTER 15
THE RIGHT DECISION

*"Good decisions come from experience. Experience comes
from making bad decisions."*
-Mark Twain

The weekend seemed to last forever. On Monday morning, Jack couldn't wait to call Davis. He dialed Davis' cell, and the Bluetooth kicked in.

"It's a good Morning at Omega," answered Davis.

Jack laughed. "That's just a bit too chipper for a Monday. You know some of us are stuck in Jersey traffic—I'm in construction traffic for the next forty-five minutes?"

"Come on. What's better than spending time with your neighbors on the road together? So, did you give any thought to which candidate to hire?" Davis asked with a grin.

"Are you kidding? It's nearly all I thought and talked about," Jack said. "My wife wants to kill me."

Davis smiled. "So, who's it going to be?"

Jack was silent a moment. "I decided on Sharon. I took your advice and inventoried my team's talents and skills. Seems to me Sharon is the best fit."

"Excellent. I guess that means she got her essay to you on time."

"It was there by the time I got home. Brett's arrived an hour later."

"Great. Check with Carol and HR then get ready to make your offer. I'll do the same with Brett. Holly will be difficult to replace but he'll be a great addition to my team."

Jack adjusted his earpiece. "I have to admit hiring on a WHIM took a bit longer than I had expected but it was time well spent. Finding these two great candidates seemed easy."

Davis laughed. "Easy? Jack I've come home from a day of interviewing without a single candidate I'd like to pursue. The better your screening upfront the better your time will be invested. Remember I've been working with Diane for years, she helps me find candidates that fit my team. And remember, even though we have two strong candidates, they may both say no. Which brings us back to our first conversation—always have a file of candidates you keep current."

"I know—always be interviewing."

"Right. You never know when an opening will come up," Davis said. "But if you follow the process, you'll increase the likelihood of finding the right candidate. That means use the timeline, listen to the resume and establish good relationships with universities, recruiters and hiring conferences. That way you're more likely to meet a Brett or a Sharon."

"Well, I'm on board with the process," Jack affirmed. "But I was wondering—do you always feel this confident when you're getting ready to extend an offer? I mean, what happens if you still have doubts and the candidate?"

"Well, it does happen," Davis admitted. "And when it does, I run through a few extra steps. First, I ask does this candidate have the foundational skill set to perform the job and then I go over each of the four qualities again and consider whether each is already present in the candidate—remember the qualities are non-teachable and non-negotiable. Jack, what would you recommend to me if I had a candidate who had three strong qualities but one weak or missing quality?"

"That's a great question. Maybe—bring him in for another interview to try and confirm if the quality is missing or not. You might also probe those areas when you call the candidate's references, or you could listen to your instincts and pass on the candidate."

"Those are all good ideas. There have been times when I've been faced with the difficult task of passing on an overall good candidate who seemed to lack one of the qualities. If possible, wait for the right one, though painful now, it will pay off in the long run."

"What would you say I took a chance or had to fill the opening and I hired that candidate you just described?"

"If you would choose to hire him then you do so with your eyes wide open. You understand that there may be a weakness for example, with his work ethic. If work ethic is the concern, then you'll need to expend a bit more energy monitoring activity and keeping a sharp eye out for issues and patterns that will need to be addressed right away. Your hope might be that he matures in this area or that you can minimize the impact of the quality in question, but you may find the role of a micro-manager unappealing and if that's not for you then it is best to pass."

Jack let out a sigh, "To hire a candidate like that would certainly be risky and more work for me because we can't teach these qualities—which is why we hire them."

"That's right. And all four need to be there. Once I've established that a candidate has them, I listen to my gut, keeping in mind what we said about instincts and insights. If I'm still uneasy, I sit on the decision to figure out what's bothering me. Then if I need to go back and clarify something with the candidate, I do. I've also sat down with another manager or colleague and shared my concerns. I find input from seasoned managers is always helpful. I'm not shy about asking for help. If I'm not sold on the person after that, I don't extend the offer."

Jack felt deflated. "Even after all that work?"

"Well, remember what we talked about. Hiring someone who isn't right for the position will be stressful and difficult for me, the company and the individual. And that's not good for anyone. And isn't that what got us here in the first place?"

"Makes sense," Jack admitted. "Well, since your advice has been solid so far, I'd like to hear your last pearl of wisdom."

Davis smiled. "Look there's no hard science to the hiring process. If anything, it's more of an art. But here's the last step. When you make Sharon the offer, let her know you're not certain it's what she wants. Though you are very excited to have her on the team, ask her to take an extra day to give her decision a last round of serious thought—to make sure this is the right fit for her. Remind her of the many benefits of working in our industry and particularly for Omega. But is this what she really wants? And does she feel her skills and talents are well-suited enough for the role? Does she see herself working for Omega—for you?"

"Wait." Jack was taken aback. "You mean you try talking the prospect out of the job again?"

"Not at all. What I'm asking is for the candidate to look carefully at the whole scenario one last time to make sure it's what she wants."

"But what happens if Sharon thinks it over and I lose her?"

"Then you've saved Sharon and yourself a lot of time and energy. If she leaves before she starts, then there must have been a disconnect or reservation, enough to for her to change her mind. And that's something you'd rather find out now. It will be a lot more painful for all concerned if you find out later."

Jack shook his head. "I guess. But I have to admit I'm nervous about doing this."

Davis nodded. "I understand, especially if this is the first time you approach the hiring process this way. But throughout my years, I've had very few who have not come back to me the next day anxious to move forward. For the candidates that decided not to move forward, though I was disappointed, it was probably a good decision for both of us. Asking them to confirm their desire to work for me actually serves the opposite purpose. At first, the candidate worries that you may doubt her suitability and that an offer like this could slip away. Then she thinks about how right the job is. Believe me, tomorrow won't come fast enough for her to assure you that she is the one for your team."

Jack signaled to turn off his exit. "I know you've been doing this awhile but are you sure it works out that way?" he questioned.

"It has worked for me. And think about it—the words you as the hiring manager most want to hear are, 'I know you're taking a chance on me, but I won't let you down. You won't be sorry.' Once you reach that point, you're ready to hire an employee you've vetted and who's committing to the organization because he's committed to you."

Jack nodded. "Ok, this sounds intriguing. I'll give it a try and see how it goes. By the way, I owe you a coffee—I mean, herbal tea—for all your help."

Davis laughed. "Just make sure that when you're a big star you remember me."

Once Jack arrived at the office, he cleared his decision with Carol Chang and HR. With Sharon's application in front of him, he called her number.

"Hello, Sharon, this is Jack Woodward from Omega Industries. I really enjoyed getting to know you and I've got some great news. I'd like to extend you an offer."

Advice on Making an Offer

One of the most exciting times in an employee/manager relationship is when an offer is made. To strengthen an employee's personal commitment and their desire to prove themselves you can use this time to reinforce their resolve.

1. When making the offer to the prospect, pull it back a bit:
This felt natural to me. If this does not fit your style and approach, then don't force it.

- After you complete the interview process and establish a solid rapport with the prospect, ask her to take a day or two to think over the offer.

- When you pull a desired item back, it often creates a greater affection for the item which can be beneficial in establishing employee commitment.

- If you ease back on your enthusiasm, it gives the candidate latitude to spend time reinforcing why the job is right for him.

- Applying the brakes to the offer a bit may also give the prospect enough time to realize this may not be the right job for her. Though having a candidate turn down an offer at the last minute might be frustrating, it is actually a blessing. Having an employee who is not committed

2. Always be recruiting because openings are often unwelcomed surprises:
- When a hire works out well, reach out to the source whether it be a college, recruiting firm or referral service and thank the appropriate people for a great hire. Strengthening relationships with these sources improves the likelihood that they will continue to funnel similar candidates to you.
    - Even if the prospect doesn't quite meet your needs now, thank the source for the referral.
- Keep a list of prospects who weren't quite right for the open position or who came just behind a superior candidate. You never know whether they might be right for a future role.
    - As I often say, "Keep in touch with number two." Number two being the candidate who came up just a bit short. What is terrific about number two is that in many cases he has been interviewed, sometimes twice, and vetted.
    - When letting a number two know that he didn't get the job, express how impressed you were with him and that

you'd like to keep in touch. "Can I reach out every few months to see what you are doing and how you are doing?"

- o These candidates may have lacked experience, professional maturity, or might have had a weak quality. When you have an opening a year later, your number twos all have more experience, professional maturity and may have had opportunity or life experiences that helped them develop their character. They should be more valuable and stronger candidates.
- o Mark my words, you will find yourself with an opening and realize that one of your number twos is ready to re-engage. The best news is, ninety percent of the interviewing process has already been completed. If you move forward with him your time-to-fill for the position will be much shorter than if you were starting out from scratch.

- Keep in contact with your sources of potential candidates even when you don't have a current opening. The stronger the relationship with the college, the recruiter or referral service the harder the staff will work for you.
  - o Offer to provide a value-added service to them. For example, help at the college's career fair, offer to conduct an informational talk on your industry or a source for career advice.
- Keep in mind that even if you make an offer to a candidate, she may not accept it:
  - o This is one reason it's crucial to always be recruiting.
  - o Keep in touch with prospects and sources even when you don't have an opening. Let them know that even though there's nothing available at the moment, you'd like to keep in touch for the future.
  - o Build and maintain a file or list of qualified screened candidates but remember that you and/or HR will need to recheck them once a need arises.
  - o Reach out to prospects periodically and ask the candidates to do the same.

3. If you have doubts about a candidate, it's better to confirm or pass on him.
   - A poor decision always has big consequences in time, money and resources.
   - If you are unsure about a quality:
     - o Schedule another interview

- o   Probe the issue when you call their references
- o   Because these qualities overlap do you see a weakness elsewhere.
- If you choose to hire a candidate, you may have doubts about remember to watch and monitor the areas of concern. This may have you playing the role of a micro-manager which for many is one to be avoided.
  - o   If you become concerned with the employee' behavior or activity level, address it immediately and have a plan to minimize the impact to the team. For example, if you are concerned about work ethic then this employee may need to turn in additional activity reports or require more of your attention until a more permanent process can be established.
  - o   Though these qualities are difficult if not impossible to teach it should not discourage a manager from demonstrating and verbally reinforcing the values and expectations you demand.

CHAPTER 16
ONBOARDING

> "Onboarding is the most important hour in an
> employee's tenure."
> -Me (Garrett Miller)

"Knock, knock," Jack poked his head into Davis's office. "Got a minute?"

"Hey, Jack. Good to see you." Davis motioned to the chair by his desk. "What brings you around so early on a Monday?"

"I'm in to meet with HR and then onboard Sharon. I'm meeting with her in about an hour."

"That's terrific." Davis grinned. "I think you found a winner. Are you still excited about her prospects?"

"Yes, I think so." Jack put his tablet on his lap. "She's been very responsive and communicative—right on track." His voice trailed off.

Davis' smartwatch chimed, signaling fifteen minutes before his phone meeting. "For a guy about to onboard the next superstar, you sure seem distracted. I've got a few minutes. Tell me what's on your mind."

Jack shifted in the chair. "To be honest, I'm worried. I mean if Sharon doesn't work out—I'm done. With my history of hiring mistakes, my boss—well you know." He paused. "It makes me wonder if I'm really cut out for managing people."

Davis nodded. "I know the feeling. But the key to being a successful manager is hiring great people and then getting out of their way. Your team already has some dynamite members and you just hired someone I think will do a fabulous job."

"That's just it," Jack said with a nod. "You have expectations. I have expectations. But what happens if Sharon doesn't live up to them?"

"Well, it's true there are no guarantees when it comes to hiring employees. But when you hire work ethic, humility, integrity, and maturity you significantly increase the chances of success, which means you also significantly reduce the risk of failure. We've done the hard work of finding and hiring WHIM. I believe Brett and Sharon are going to do great. Today is an exciting day. You should be excited as you help Sharon launch her career." Davis paused. "To be honest, the onboarding process is my favorite time as a manager."

Jack tapped at his tablet with the stylus. Suddenly, he felt back in unfamiliar territory. "I don't get it. Why would onboarding be your favorite time? For me, it was a day of filling out paperwork, listening to HR drone on about healthcare, expense reports, being issued an employee handbook I have yet to look at and reading through a lot of policies and procedures."

Davis laughed. "Sounds familiar. But you left out my favorite part. The big reveal."

"Big reveal? What is HR not covering?"

"The big reveal is why I hired Brett. This is when I pull back the curtain and introduce him to WHIM and why I believe WHIM has been the key to his success so far and why I believe it will be the key to his success in the future. This is a time for me to build him up and set expectations."

Jack pressed the screen of his tablet. "Okay, this sounds interesting. Tell me more."

Davis smiled. "Glad you asked. First, I see the discussion as the most critical time you'll spend with Sharon or any new employee because you're reinforcing what you believe are the keys to success. You know why you hired Sharon, but she doesn't. Here's where you let her in on what WHIM is and that she has the qualities you were looking for. Unpack WHIM for her. Define the qualities—what they sounded like and looked like during the interview. You'll see her beam with pride. It happens every time."

Jack shrugged. "Okay, everyone loves to be complimented."

Davis shook his head. "It's more than that. We hire based on the concept that past performance is the best predictor of future performance and that Sharon's example of WHIM qualities before the interview is what you expect during her tenure with the company—"

"I think I get it," Jack put in. "I'm basically telling Sharon why I hired her and what I expect more of."

"Right," Davis affirmed. "But you're also communicating something even more valuable. "You're pulling back the camera and giving Sharon the bigger picture of your team, which will be built around WHIM. Help Sharon see and understand what the qualities look like on your team and at Omega."

Jack stopped typing and reread what he wrote. "So, am I going so far as to define each of the WHIM traits? Maybe paint a picture of what each looks like on my team?"

"Great idea. And pause once in a while as you're talking. Make sure Sharon's taking notes. And make sure she not only understands how you've defined WHIM but agrees with the definitions."

Jack looked up. "Can you expand on what you mean by agrees?"

Davis smiled. "Glad you picked up on the nuance because this is where we as managers get it wrong. Too often we make statements and don't check to see if our audience understands and buys into the value of our insights. By way of example, this short conversation between you and me will be the foundation on which your future coaching with Sharon and all your employees is built upon."

Jack made a note. "So, do you talk about WHIM with your team and employees as openly as you're talking about it with me?"

Davis nodded. "This is how I coach—all the time. You can talk with one of my employees to verify it. Once we define and agree on WHIM, we can begin the path forward. In my experience, almost every point of friction I've had with an employee boils down to an issue of WHIM."

Jack made another note. "So, what I'm doing is setting expectations. Sharon will know what I'm looking for and expect. And I'll know she understands what I'm expecting—and why." Jack tapped out a few more notes then stopped.

Davis looked over the desk. "Is there something you don't agree with?"

"No. I just can't believe I've never had an introductory conversation around my expectations. Not one with this depth anyway. I've just always assumed my new hires understood what I wanted and expected from them and why—bad assumption. It's hard not to feel a little foolish."

Davis smiled. "Easy, there. You're only foolish if you don't learn from the past and change your methods." He sat forward. "So, let me share one last insight—expectation is the key word here. One of my truisms is that we're sad when our expectations aren't met and happy when our expectations are exceeded. If that's true, and I believe it is, then setting expectations is the key."

Jack nodded. "As you were talking, I was just thinking about past hires I quickly became frustrated with because they weren't working or acting as I'd hoped." He shook his head. "But it wasn't their fault. It was mine. I never communicated what I was looking for or why. I guess I never knew." He smiled. "But I know now."

Davis looked at his watch. "Perfect timing because I need to jump on a conference call. Feeling better?"

"Definitely," Jack said with a nod. "I have half an hour before I meet with Sharon." He got up from the chair. "I'm going to use the time to write out a list of definitions and expectations." He tucked his tablet under his arm. "And I'm really grateful for your insights. I can see why this is one of the most important times in an employee's career." He pocketed his phone and held out his hand out to his mentor. "And I probably have you to thank for my future success, not to mention my sanity." He smiled. "I'm not sure which is more important."

Davis grinned. "No worries. I'll just take ten percent of your yearly bonus in large bills. Seriously, keep up the good work." He pressed his earbud and gave Jack a thumbs-up.

Jack gave a wave and went out the door. This was exactly what he needed, he thought, a way to get from the interview phase to life with a promising new employee and an energized team.

The Most Important 60 Minutes

Onboarding is an oft-overlooked time that a manager cedes to HR. Make this a significant time to reveal to the new employee why she was hired. Share with her how each quality was represented during her interview process and which traits, activities, experiences, and answers stood out to you. Keep your comments job-related. These qualities do overlap into a person's personal life so be disciplined about how WHIM is reflected in the workplace.

1. Schedule time for an onboarding discussion:
   - The goal of this discussion is to introduce your team's culture to your new employee and to define WHIM and how WHIM relates to your expectations.
   - This is also a good time to hear her expectations of the position and the organization. Understand each candidate is also evaluating you and your organization and they too are hoping you and the organization display these qualities. Whether they have heard of WHIM or not, these qualities are appealing to every candidate.
     o Tie the organization's commitment to WHIM to each of her expectations.
   - The clearer you express your expectations to your new hire the less likelihood there will be of significant friction surrounding unmet expectations in the future.
   - Having this discussion upfront will give you, as the manager, a reference should there be performance issues in the future. If the onboarding process is done correctly, the employee should be able to understand which quality is in question and why.

2. Define WHIM:
   - Whenever you have a conversation with an employee, it's always helpful to define terms. If there's no agreement on terms and their definitions, there will be misunderstanding and friction when the concepts are discussed.
   - Put together a list of terms and their definitions and their contexts for your employee to commit to memory and let him know these will be referred to often during his tenure.

3. Share with your new employee what WHIM looks and sounds like in the workplace and on your team:
   - Once the terms have been defined bring the concepts to life by

giving real-life examples.

  o For instance, a manager might share what work ethic looks like: "It's as simple as helping to clean up after a meeting, arriving five minutes before a meeting begins, turning in assignments on time or early, never settling for good enough, to offering to help a colleague who is in need of assistance—assuming you are able."

  ▪ This is also a good time to share an expectation such as, "Though we have a cleaning service in our organization, they are not here to pick up after grown adults. I expect each of my team members to pick up after themselves and, having met you and seen your work ethic, I'm sure that fits in perfectly with how you conduct yourself."

  o Here are examples of what work ethic sounds like: "I'd be glad to help." "Here, let me lend a hand." "Let's try and get this right before we submit it." "Good enough never is."

4. The candidate's WHIM:

This is the big reveal. Letting a candidate know the criteria on which they were hired is rarely if ever discussed. "Do you know why I hired you?" is the beginning to a powerful and encouraging conversation.

  • Onboarding is a great time to reveal to the candidate that you hired him because of the WHIM traits you saw during the interview process.

  • Review the specifics from the prospect's interview and resume that displayed these impressive qualities.

  • Emphasize your expectation to see the qualities consistently expressed during his tenure.

5. WHIM is not only a hiring criterion but part of your team's culture:

  • Your desire is that these qualities should always be what defines those on the team.

  • It is the manager and his team's responsibility to demonstrate and encourage WHIM in others.

  • Empower the employee to respectfully also hold you accountable to these ideals.

6. Defining WHIM now sets the tone for coaching in the future:

  • If you've set the WHIM tone and parameters in advance, the employee will expect to hear WHIM during midyear and end-of-

year reviews as well as during coaching sessions.
- Remember, what we expect we must inspect.

7. What if there is a weak or missing quality?
If by chance or necessity, you hired a candidate who may be missing a quality, or who has a weak quality, or who has a quality you could not confirm during the interview process this is a great opportunity.
- By reviewing in detail each of the qualities, you are also setting expectations.
- If for example, a candidate's humility was in question take time to:
  - Define humility.
    - Make sure you get agreement on how humility is defined.
    - State what humility looks like in the workplace and on your team. Give lots of examples
      - Willingness to ask questions, to seek advice, receive correction, listen to others, place others before self, and to be a life-long learner.
    - State what humility sounds like in the workplace and on your team. Give lots of examples.
      - "Thank you for the feedback, please let me know how I can improve? I'm sorry I interrupted you. Please, you go first. How did you learn to do that so well? Yes, I'm always open to being better."
    - Ask if the new employee agrees and maybe can give you examples of how they have lived humility out in his life or last job
- Now that you have defined each of the qualities the employee is aware of what you will be expecting and monitoring.
- If there are any gaps, hopefully the employee will be more aware of their needs. At the very least if there is an issue that arises due to this concern it will not be a surprise to the employee.

CHAPTER 17
SHORING UP THE FOUNDATION

"An ounce of prevention is worth a pound of cure."
-Benjamin Franklin

The musical ringtone jarred Davis from pouring over the month's sales figures. He shook his head to free his thoughts and glanced at the display. "Jack, long time, no chat. Hope all is well. I see you're calling from Boston."

"Yes, and all's well here. The traffic is Boston is no better than the traffic in Jersey but it's a great time to make phone calls. How are you?"

"I'm great but always trying to improve."

Jack paused. "Say ... how's your new hire working out?"

"Brett's terrific, just as I'd anticipated. But is that concern I hear in your voice? Everything all right with Sharon?"

"Sharon's great, miles ahead of where my last few hires were three months into the job. She's also had a positive impact on the team." Jack paused again.

Davis sat forward. "Now I know I hear concern. What's on your mind?"

"Well, you know I'm a believer in hiring WHIM. And I know the importance of hiring employees who already have a solid work ethic, humility, integrity, and maturity. I've seen it work and I'm proud of my first WHIM hire. But a recent news event really hit me. The story has me thinking maybe WHIM is too good to be true, that it's flawed."

Davis closed his laptop. "Well, you certainly have my attention—and my curiosity. I'm open to having my ideas challenged and tested. So, I'm curious. What has you flustered? Your feedback could be helpful."

"Did you see the story about the four-star general caught in an extramarital affair?" Jack paused. "I mean, he was a four-star. If anyone had

WHIM he did, right? He graduated from West Point near the top of his class, was promoted and served for decades with distinction. Then this happens. What happened to his foundation, his WHIM DNA?"

Davis' smile faded. He could hear the depth of concern in Jack's voice. "I'm familiar with the story and you're right. It's devastating. When a leader and good example fails, it shakes our faith in people. We wonder if that can happen to good men and women, what about others, what about us?"

"Exactly. I find myself thinking that if a guy who had WHIM can fall, what hope does my last hire have? And what hope do I have of maintaining these qualities in myself?"

Davis nodded. "I know how you feel. If you've got a few minutes, I'll share an experience that shaped my thinking on the issue."

Jack smiled. "A few minutes? Did I mention I was in Boston traffic? I'm all ears."

Davis turned and looked out the window. "When I was in college, I worked as a mason's helper for my boss, Tom. We built chimneys, stone walls, patios, and foundations. And we poured concrete floors. Overall, it wasn't a stressful line of work—unless we were pouring a floor."

"I would have guessed climbing scaffolding and walking up and down roofs two or three stories high would have been the most stressful part," Jack said with a grin. "Why pouring floors?"

"After we poured the concrete into the forms we had to put on a smooth finish before the concrete hardened." Davis smiled. "To me, a perfectly smooth concrete floor is a sight of beauty. And under the right conditions, it's not hard to do. But can you guess what were we working against?"

Jack glanced at his cell. "Time?"

"Right. Now add a blazing hot sun and a Connecticut shoreline breeze."

Jack nodded. "So, time and the elements. How can you keep concrete from drying too fast under those conditions?"

Davis grinned. "Now you're starting to feel the anxiety of pouring a floor. While Tom was smoothing the surface, I lightly wet the unfinished parts to slow the drying process and keep the surface malleable. Eventually, time and the elements would win out and the concrete would set."

"You mean it would dry unfinished? What then?"

"At that point, there was nothing we could do," Davis said. "If we didn't get a smooth surface on the floor before it set, we failed. Once concrete sets, I could use a fire hose to wet the floor, but it would never become soft again. WHIM is the same way. As we mature, our WHIM qualities are set, like concrete. For the most part, those qualities won't change much. They may mature a bit but that's about all."

"Okay, I understand the analogy. But why would great people with all the qualities in place falter to the point of self-destruction? It doesn't make sense. You either have WHIM or not, right?"

"Well, yes, but hear me out. While I was working as a mason, Tom and I spent a lot of time building strong, almost immovable structures. But we also spent a lot of time repairing and shoring up structures that at one time appeared indestructible. You must have seen cracks in a foundation or sidewalk. What did you notice about them?"

"I think I know where you're headed," Jack put in. "Cracks often start small but left unattended they grow."

"That's the pattern we saw, especially in New England where structures cycle through a freezing and thawing process that repeated itself not just over years but in a single season—"

"You mean like the pothole I just hit? When a crack is left alone it will spread, get bigger and eventually compromise the structure." Jack sat quietly for a moment putting the pieces together. "All right, I get it. WHIM may be set but it still has to be maintained."

"Precisely. Whether we're talking about our employees or ourselves we're dealing with fallible humans, aren't we? Lord knows I have my flaws."

"You?" Jack grinned. "I can't believe your foundation has any imperfections."

"Nobody's perfect. And remember the primary teacher of WHIM is life events. The qualities of work ethic, humility, integrity, and maturity are molded in our youth but over time and under stress they can weaken. That's another reason I don't hire someone who's missing even one of these qualities. I may be a good manager, but I can't control life. And I'm not willing to bet that one day a life event will teach WHIM to a newly hired employee. Life events and circumstances will batter the walls and foundations of WHIM, which means we have to be vigilant about maintaining and repairing our foundations."

"So, you're saying this general had cracks that weren't addressed and spread to the point where the structure was compromised?"

"Right. So, if I gave you the impression you could hire based on the WHIM model and you'd be done I didn't paint the full picture. WHIM provides the building blocks for a great employee, but managers have to do more than just hire the qualities, they must also create and maintain a WHIM culture. Fixing spider cracks is relatively easy. Repairing a breached foundation is a lot more complicated."

Jack tapped the display of his cell. He was afraid to ask the next question, but he had to get an answer. "Can a cracked WHIM foundation be repaired?"

"In my experiences, both in concrete and in life, the smaller the crack the easier the repair. The good news is that there's hope. Redemption is a beautiful process. It just takes hard work. Twenty years after we bought our house, I noticed water damage that had probably started just after the being built. The flashing was incorrectly installed and twenty years later a small fix turned into a major repair. So, too, with relationships. The damage may be extensive, but if both parties are willing restoration is possible." Davis paused a moment. "Jack, are you there? I didn't lose you, did I?"

"No, I'm here. You're saying it's easier to maintain a foundation than rebuild it. But it's still comforting to know that foundations can be repaired."

"Exactly. When I slip up, I stop, try and process what went wrong then look to learn from it and move on. I keep my eye on the prize—to live and model WHIM for my family, friends, and associates. It's not easy."

Jack sighed. "Okay, but I'm still feeling a little overwhelmed. Am I supposed to look for the spider cracks in myself and all my direct reports?"

Davis laughed. "You're not called to be everyone's conscience and guardian. I've tried that and it's terrible for all parties. Instead, use and incorporate the language of WHIM to strengthen your team's culture. Keep it top of mind for them—talk about it in the lunchroom, at meetings, during field rides, and during presentations. Make it part of the review process and for a 360-degree perspective make sure you seek your team's feedback and input on your WHIM qualities. Ask if they see spider cracks in you that you may not be aware of."

"Come to think of it I guess I already began the process. I followed your advice while onboarding Sharon, so the WHIM language and expectations are already familiar to her. I've also begun working WHIM into my oral and written communications," Jack affirmed. "But I haven't yet used it in our review process or coaching sessions. That shouldn't be difficult."

"It isn't," Davis agreed. "I also found where WHIM and Omega's principles intersect. That also helps intertwine these qualities into their corporate life. Let me send you the document." He paused and made a note. "Meanwhile, keep up with all you're doing because you're on your way to creating a sustainable culture. Speak of WHIM often and it will become the way your people define the team and themselves. Have them speak of the team's culture with pride."

"You mean with humility, don't you?" Jack said with a laugh. "Seriously, this is where humility is really valuable. The manager and the employee both need to have it to properly give and receive feedback."

"Right, humility is essential to maintaining a healthy culture. To coach and graciously receive coaching are the oil that keeps the feedback mechanism running. But don't forget about the rest of WHIM. Each quality plays a role."

"Well, integrity is needed if I'm to be honest about my weaknesses and my assessments of others. And both parties need maturity to have the right emotional response as they give and receive feedback. If either party lacks maturity and becomes defensive, angry, hurt, offended, or insulted, it could derail the entire process.

"Exactly. As to work ethic, it's the willingness to do the hard work of maintaining the foundations. It's easier in the short run to ignore a problem and figure you'll address or fix it later. But a solid work ethic doesn't let things slide. It recognizes the crack and commits to a repair, and to having the uncomfortable conversation to avoid the really difficult conversation later. It also includes the hard work of evaluating our foundations."

"Got it." Jack hesitated. "But people can be blind to their worst habits and traits. Even if I look, I still might not see my weak points."

"Well, here's the million-dollar question. What good is having amazing qualities if they slip away? The answer is two-fold. First, we always need to be open and ready to receive correction and build an environment that promotes honest communication. That's part of humility. Second, since I can't always count on others to be forthright, I have a few people in my life who are candid with me. I've given them the permission and the challenge of helping keep me honest."

Jack paused. "I'm not sure I have those types of relationships."

"It may take work to create the right bonds but those with WHIM tend to gravitate toward others who possess it. Look for those people and foster those relationships. My most prized fan and critic is my wife. She reads me like a book and is honest with me. I don't know where I'd be without her."

"Come to think of it, I have a friend who's brutally honest with me, too," Jack said. "I don't go to him for a pick-me-up, that's for sure. But at least I know he'll tell me what I need to hear."

"Right, those friends are like canaries in a coal mine. They help prevent disaster, in this case for us, our teams and our families."

"It's an early warning system, like your gas light blinking, which, by the way, I've ignored too many times," Jack said with a grin.

"Everyone has. But there's another motivation to encouraging WHIM in my life and on my team. Not only am I building a low-maintenance team, but I'm also helping insulate myself, my team, and the organization from unnecessary struggles. Architects design strong foundations not only to support the structure but also for protection and to preserve the integrity of the footprint. Hiring and maintaining WHIM in our culture adds protection and security from a lot of the issues that plague organizations, such as problems with integrity, pride, communication, teamwork, engagement, and accountability, just to name a few."

"All right, so how do I encourage my associates to develop these relationships?" Jack asked. "I'll bet the general wishes he had a few people in his life who might have challenged him."

"Right, so start by helping each person to see that no one's immune to the stresses we've been talking about. The news is full of examples of individuals or organizations that chose not to repair or acknowledge cracks or shortcomings. Use these as small case studies and have your team share their thoughts on what actions the subjects could have taken to have prevented the poor outcomes. You'll want to also find stories of people or organizations who recognized the cracks and invested the time and resources to make the needed repairs which allowed them to avert a disaster and thrive. Sharing examples will keep these concepts alive and practical."

"Just having this conversation has inspired me to give my friend a call," Jack affirmed.

"Perfect. And to help evaluate whether your employees have this type of friend in their lives they can ask themselves this question: 'When was the last time a friend corrected me or told me something that touched a nerve, and how did I respond?' If they can't recall a time when they were corrected and responded positively, they need to look for and foster the kind of relationship that will enable that to happen. If they have a person they can be open with, they need to buy that friend a coffee and have him or her ask some hard questions about each WHIM quality."

"I'm way ahead of you. It's time to phone a friend. Wait—" Jack paused. "I think I already did."

"What do you mean?"

"Well, when it comes to a business mentor, you've been that person."

Davis smiled. "I guess you're right. The time we've spent was so natural it didn't really feel like work. I'm honored."

"So far, it's been mostly a one-way relationship," Jack said with a grin. "But I'm better off for it. Hopefully, one day I'll return the favor."

"Jack, these relationships are always a two-way street. Whenever I give advice or encourage someone, I'm speaking as much to myself as to the other person. I can't tell you how often I've conducted a personal inventory before or after I've challenged a friend. It's never a one-way exchange."

Jack laughed. "Great. I'm glad I've given you so many opportunities for self-reflection. Hang in there and I'll have more where they came from."

"Anytime, my friend. Listen, I have to run but let's talk again soon."

Jack said goodbye then took a few moments to think through the call. His GPS let him know he was near his exit. He thought about the beating his ego had taken while Davis was helping him through the hiring process, but in the back of his mind he always knew Davis had his best interests at heart. Jack wanted to make sure he fostered that same transparency and trust with his team.

Jack exited the highway and pulled up to a red light. His mind was racing thinking about all the ways he could incorporate the language and ideas into his team's culture. He glanced over at the massive building across the street and thought about its foundation. You must build upon a sure foundation, a solid rock, and with that thought, the light turned green.

Maintaining WHIM

One of the very first questions asked of me when I returned to an organization for a follow-up class was, 'I hired my first WHIM candidate. What now?" I realized that the importance of creating a culture of WHIM was necessary to maintain everyone's foundations.

1. Always set the example of WHIM:
   - When you've fallen short of your standards, conduct a quick self-assessment as to how, when, and why this occurred. Then bounce the scenario off a trusted friend or colleague. Look for patterns and introduce an ounce of prevention to help address the cracks.
   - The more transparent and honest you are in your assessments, the greater the opportunity for growth.
   - Never be afraid to admit a mistake. It shows humility and creates an atmosphere of accountability.

2. Use WHIM wherever appropriate to describe your organization's culture:
   - Review your organization's core values, integrity statements, and mission statements, and tie the qualities of WHIM into them.

3. Use WHIM language during midyear and year-end reviews:
   - Performance reviews are a great time to evaluate an employee's work ethic, humility, integrity, and maturity. Incorporating these qualities and concepts into the review process is the best way to cement them into the organization's culture. Employees will pay attention to the qualities if they expect to see, discuss, and consistently be measured by them. Reviews should revolve around important character components, as well as performance. The consistent expression of good character is what helps propel performance and promote a strong team and company culture.
   - These questions and checkpoints might be helpful to include during a review:
     o How has the employee's performance and work ethic compared with that of his counterparts?
     o Evaluate how successfully the employee has completed the administrative responsibilities associated with his position.
     o Does the employee have a track record for being prompt to meetings and appointments and for completing tasks on or ahead of time?
     o How well has the employee embraced and completed her

personal development plans?

- o When the employee is self-evaluating her performance, is she able to accurately assess her development and progress? Is she willing to ask for help?
- o As the manager looks back at interactions throughout the year, how does the employee respond to public and/or private correction?
- o Evaluate the employee's relationships with his customers and colleagues. Do you find that any have become strained or improved during the evaluation timeframe? If so, why? If the relationship is strained or has improved, how has he affected the relationship? If strained what are his plans to repair or improve the relationship?
- o Does the employee have a reputation for being defensive or argumentative, or is he easy to work with? Use examples.
- o Is the employee credible, and does she create an atmosphere of trust?
- o Have there been any concerns about his integrity? What are the concerns, and are they legitimate and substantiated?
- o Does the employee have a reputation for being easy to work with and a team player? Have there been times of angry outbursts, being easily offended, and/or being overly defensive when challenged?
- o Is the employee accountable for her mistakes or is she quick to offer excuses for performance concerns?
- o What were the employee's greatest struggles, failures, or regrets this past year, and how did she respond to each? Has she learned from the events and expressed gratitude for the lessons learned? Has she considered what she would have done differently? Is her posture one of defensiveness, finger-pointing, and blaming? Or can she accept responsibility for her role in the process?
- o What is the employee most proud of this year? What are her greatest achievements and wins? What did she learn from these successes? How can she use these successes to continue her growth?

4. Use WHIM language during employee coaching sessions:
   - When coaching a team, use WHIM descriptors in daily conversation.
   - Use WHIM language when you're discussing strategy, development, customers, career planning, or reviewing objectives

for a project.

- Instead of focusing on a consistently late expense report, focus instead on work ethic, a common and clear understanding of the time commitment required for these duties, and the importance of meeting deadlines, for both the individual and the team.
- Use WHIM language to praise and recognize expressions of these qualities.

5. Use real-life examples of WHIM successes and missteps:
   - History is replete with examples of good people and organizations who have let their guard down, made poor judgments and suffered the consequences. Use these as examples to help reinforce the benefits of WHIM with your team.
     - o These examples remind each person that a reputation can be damaged in moments.
   - There are countless excellent examples of people and organizations who have excelled while maintaining WHIM qualities. Give examples of those with support networks that kept them grounded and centered. Encourage employees to develop these types of relationships and help them understand how to do this.

6. When trust is breached, seek a way to repair the damage and restore the relationship:
   - One of the most difficult tasks in any relationship is to heal and repair the effects of a betrayal. Not addressing the relationship breach, however, will only lead to further deterioration. All employees must recognize when a relationship has been damaged and pursue reconciliation.
   - To repair a damaged relationship, avoid using or accepting the oft-abused phrase, "I'm sorry." Using this phrase may not address or uncover the issues at hand. Over the years I've developed this used this three-step process for seeking reconciliation:
     - o First, the offender must acknowledge that he has done something wrong and accept responsibility for it. This is best done by the offender describing the offense. Hearing the description of the offense assures the offended party that the right issue is being addressed and acknowledged.
     - o Second, the offending party must then state what should have been done instead, for example: "Chris, I lied about why I handed my report in late and need to ask your forgiveness. I should have come to you earlier in the week and let you know I was struggling with the project. It

won't happen again. Do you forgive me?"

- o The third step involves the offended party granting the forgiveness that completes the process. Be patient during this last stage, as the relationship may remain sensitive while restoration takes its course:
  - The step is important because if the offended party holds a grudge, a root of bitterness will grow and be detrimental to the relationship. It will also eventually poison all other relationships involving the two parties.
- This three-step process goes a long way to repairing relationships that have been damaged and requires both parties to be vulnerable. When the goal is to repair the relationship, there can be no pride on either side.
- If both parties don't engage in the process, there will be little hope of repairing the problem, and the relationship will continue to sour and suffer from trust issues.

7. Fix the spider cracks:
   - Don't let cracks form in your, your team's or your organization's foundation; cracks will spread. Left unattended, cracks will lead to further degradation.
   - Whether you're a manager or an employee, find a friend to hold you accountable for repairing and strengthening the area(s) in question.
   - The saying, "Pride goes before a fall," refers to this scenario. People who are too proud to ask for help are most vulnerable to a character crisis, thus exposing their foundation to possible damage.
   - Stay humble and ask help from people you trust. Your reputation depends on it.

COLLEGE RECRUITING
BY JIM THRASHER

"It's all about relationships."
-Dr. Jim Thrasher

Mike, a recruiter for a major corporation, approached a new year of recruiting at a large university hoping to find a diamond in the rough. In preparation, his company filled out the on-campus recruiting information form for the Career Services office. As a routine exercise, the company's HR staff listed the name of the recruiter coming on the firm's behalf either as "TBA" or "Will Advise." This left the option open for the company to send either of its two college recruiters, Mike or Rich. Mike would be returning this year for the fifth time.

Mike arrived at the Career Services office ready to go. He was greeted by the recruiter coordinator and responded, "Hi, Rosemary. How are you? I'm—" As he tried to reintroduce himself, she said, "It is nice to see you again, Will."

At first, Mike was confused at being called "Will." He shook his head as he began to say "I'm not Will, I'm—"

Again, Rosemary interrupted. "Oh! I hope nothing has happened to Mr. Advise!"

Incredulous, many thoughts flashed through Mike's mind.

Finally, he reflected, How sad! This is a university we've tried for years to build a corporate relationship with, yet our efforts haven't been reciprocated. It's apparent we've been unsuccessful in the most basic sense.

But Mike bit his tongue and was ushered by Rosemary into the interview room, never to see a career services person that day. The candidate interviews, too, were less than productive. Out of the ten students who signed up, there were four no-shows, five solid "noes" and only one candidate worth considering. Mike drove back to the hotel, his mentor's often-repeated maxim ringing in his ears: "It's all about relationships." Personal, sincere relationships will bring forth the exceptional candidates.

Mike shared this story with his colleagues back at the office, and from that time on, he has been affectionately called "Will" or "Mr. Advise" by nearly the entire company.

Recruiting Is More of an Art, Than a Science

I often say to the hundreds of recruiters who come to our campus each year that what they do is an art, not a science. I have the utmost respect for what these professionals accomplish in their management and HR roles. They take in multiple pieces of information about students—impressions and intuitions that are of different shapes and colors. They then align these puzzle pieces and assess the "fit" of the newly formed picture. Wow! What a knack! What a gift! What an opportunity, and what a responsibility! These recruiters are defining their companies' futures, one individual at a time. The role they play within their firms is exceedingly important.

When there are literally thousands of puzzle pieces—pieces that might fit into a corporate frame—scattered across the nation, where do these hiring professionals look first? How do they most effectively use their time and resources to search for those few pieces that have just the right pattern? Through relationships: ties to trusted placement offices that can gather the best pieces for recruiters to examine, test, and see whether they fit.

It may take a little work to develop relationships on campus, but the payoff can be substantial. An alumnus of our college recruited on campus for a national corporation for years. She was promoted to a different position, and in the transition, the healthy relationship that had been cultivated through the years was lost. In an effort to continue the corporate relationship after she left, the former recruiter put me in touch with the company's director of college recruiting. I began calling the director the summer before the recruiting season started. Five months of follow-up calls finally persuaded him to schedule a spring day of interviewing. It was apparent that he had little interest in coming for a visit. I'll never forget that early spring morning when he arrived. Lake-effect snow had made the drive tedious, and he was not pleased. My hope was that the thirteen candidates he would soon meet would change his outlook.

At the end of the day, he came to my office and asked to speak with me. He had a confession to make. "Jim, I came to your campus for one reason today, and that was to eliminate you from my recruiting schedule. When you called, I thought, why do I want to go to a small school in rural PA? But I must admit this place has blown me away. On my best days of recruiting, I may only invite one or two recruits back, but I'm considering inviting seven or eight of your students for a second interview. I don't do that at any other campus in the country. This has been a fantastic experience; I'm grateful you so persistently coaxed me to recruit. Can I come back next year?"

This isn't primarily a story about the quality of Grove City students; it's an example of what happens when your company has a strong relationship with Career Services. Based on our years of experience with this particular firm, we had a solid understanding of the type and quality of candidates it interviewed and hired, so we were able to pick several people we thought would fit. The result is that the recruiter wasn't blindly searching and hoping for a fit; he had real potential in hand. His job got a lot easier, and his efforts were far more effective.

In other examples, a major bank on the East Coast recognized its need to reorganize its entire HR approach. They came to us first to get our feedback on their new vision and direction for recruiting. They wanted us to be a primary partner in their new recruiting endeavor. Why? Because of the great relationship we have with them.

Our deep relationships allow us to serve our customers more effectively; we know their needs and likes, and they know the services we can provide. When the Princeton Review Guide ranked our office as one of the top 12 Career Services offices in the nation three times since the ranking's inception in 2019, I was asked, why the success? Relationships.

We are a campus of only 2,500 students, yet a number of national and international colleges and universities have sought us out for advice as they reorganized their own career services departments. They, too, wanted to serve their students and corporations by providing a more efficient and effective recruiting experience. What were they seeking? The keys to building personal, sincere, and deep relationships with the corporate representatives and students they serve.

I'm asked about the role of online recruiting all the time. Certainly, online recruiting has some distinct advantages, but we have found that what has always been true remains true: Personal and dependable relationships drive the whole process of effective recruiting.

Relationships. Face-to-face relationships. It's that simple.

So, how does a hiring manager/recruiter develop highly profitable relationships with colleges and universities? Relationships are built over years. Here is an outline and a template of how to establish and build that relationship in a three-step process:

- Step 1: Appraise
- Step 2: Court
- Step 3: Partner

Step 1: Appraise

Evaluate

Think about the mission of your organization and evaluate how it fits with that of a particular university or college. One of my most highly esteemed recruiters believes this is the most important factor in getting "plugged in" and making things happen on campus. To this end, do some front-end research and reconnaissance. Ask around, look at the Career Services section of the website, attend a few campus events, or stop in one of the cafeterias for lunch before establishing contact with the Career Services office. You can tell a lot about a campus through the lens of a dining hall. Student dress, conduct, and attitudes will give you a good look at some important factors about the campus and its students, and it will give you an initial sense of whether these factors meet your work environment.

Assess

Don't remove your assessment glasses when you approach possible colleges. First impressions give an accurate read of the office and its perspective. You will know almost immediately whether to develop a relationship with the school. When I make contact with new employers/recruiters, my efforts on their behalf are immediate! My excitement to seek their best interests is apparent. We deem it a privilege, not a right, to work with each of our companies.

If from the initial phone call or email (I still recommend a phone call), the response is lukewarm or cool, or if the Career Services office takes days to get back to you, don't waste your time. There is a method to their madness. Many Career Services' barometers are based on the amount of work each relationship will demand. If an office doesn't have students coming in, or if it discourages organizations from being involved on campus, the workload is reduced significantly. This scenario does occur, and it's more prevalent than you might imagine.

Don't assume that the level or extent of services will be the same on all campuses you approach. Seek a Career Services office that is sold on the idea of your success. If you and your organization aren't appreciated and cared for right from the start, list some postings with that office to test the waters, but don't invest precious time.

When you find an office that warrants the effort, treat it as your customer. Spend time with the staff as part of your assessment. Get to know everyone. Stop in, buy them coffee at the student union, and bring in donuts and bagels. In essence, interview the staff to see what makes them tick.

Ask

When you're starting or renewing a relationship with a college Career Services office, ask the staff specific questions up front, such as:

- How many on-campus recruiting visits did you have last year?
- Could you send me a list of those companies?
- What is the student traffic like in your office regarding numbers and types of students?
- How well do you get to know your students?
- Would you be willing to be my envoy with other key campus individuals as I build a network here?
- Do you have a recruiter guide that you could send me that outlines how to get plugged into your campus?
- Will you allow me to prescreen all the candidates I might like to interview?

☐ Do your offices have available Wi-Fi and high-speed internet so that I can keep up with what's going on in my office and get work done?

Also, ask yourself some questions about the office staff. Why are they in this job? Are they biding their time, waiting for something better? Are they all about impersonally throwing resources at students, with the message, "Have at it, and I hope it goes well"? Does the staff have a passion for their work? Is there a feeling of energy? What about a commitment to serve? Does the office provide assistance without being prodded, and does the staff quickly respond to your emails and requests?

In essence, use the same perceptive approach to assess the dynamics of the career services office that you use when interviewing students. You're looking for a few key schools with which to develop deep and lasting relationships. There are exceptional candidates on every campus, but you need the right tools and help from the right people to dig deep to find them.

Expect

Set high expectations and standards as you seek a school in which to make a significant investment. You're highly perceptive; it's your business! You're not looking for the "ivory tower" in Career Services; you're looking for an efficient, customer-focused business approach to recruiting.

Time spent off-task is a significant concern for recruiters. The problems, issues, phone calls, and emails don't stop because you're out of the office interviewing. Just as you are trying to hire individuals who fit your organization, you're also trying to find career services people who are fulfilling their calling. You want professionals who love serving students and employers, and who are sincerely appreciative of your commitment to them. These are the relationships that will become profitable for you.

Step 2: Court

Identify

Develop a wide variety of relationships on campus, and identify the administrators, faculty, staff, and coaches who know the students best and have invested their lives in them. Create a network of individuals that will refer the best of the best to you. The members of this network will be your advocates with the students. You want them to funnel the most appropriate prospective recruits to you.

The right people on campus know the right students for you, so tap into their knowledge and standing on campus. These are the people to whom the students go. They are the faculty members who have great professional and personal relationships with students, the coaches who know their players outside practice. The students know who these "impact players" are on campus. They know who truly cares for them and who is devoted to them. You need to find this out, too, so do your groundwork. Ask your recent hires and the alumni who work for your organization to give you the inside scoop on identifying these key individuals.

Attract

Alumni are like magnets—use them to attract interest. Company employees who are alumni, especially recent grads from the college where you're recruiting, are great assets. A capable, well-respected student who comes on board with your company will talk at length with campus friends, and their time at your organization has been an excellent experience, he or she will talk up your company. This is priceless advertising for the opportunity and your firm.

Use recent alumni when you interview on campus. Allow the alum to greet and sit with candidates before and after the interview in the reception area. The alum isn't formally interviewing the candidates, but he or she can play a key role by making candidates feel comfortable, explaining the inside track on the position and the company, and acting as another set of eyes to evaluate the "fit."

Step 3: Partner

Engage

Engage those on-campus advocates! Get to know faculty members in specific academic departments and be prepared for the reality that many faculty members are unique people. The academic world attracts personalities from A to Z, and it may take time to build rapport and a trust relationship.

You're looking for faculty members who have an excellent teaching reputation but who also command the respect of students. You want those who are advocates for students beyond the classroom. Ask around; start with your Career Services point person, and go from there. Once you've had time on campus and some substantial student interaction, ask the students themselves. Word travels fast about college employees who really care.

Invest

Here are some ways that you can "invest" in the selected career services office.

☐ Sponsor events on campus and invest in some specific programs. One of our recruiters seeking marketing and sales candidates sponsored a business marketing class competition with a cash award for winners. The company identified a super candidate who won the prize. A year later, the candidate was hired by the company. His gifts had already been identified, and the company had an opportunity to showcase itself; a wonderful connection was made!

☐ Recruiters have also offered to start and be a member of a marketplace advisory group to advise the related academic department on market trends and information. One recruiter sponsored the inception of a national professional sales student honorary organization on campus and offered to help get it off the ground.

☐ Maybe you or a company colleague could speak on campus. Academic topics are great for the classroom, but other ideas include interviewing, resumes, cover letters, career fairs, and behavioral approaches to interviewing.

☐ Volunteer to do mock interviews for the career services office—these are opportunities to show students what you wish candidates would do in an interview.

☐ Offer to provide products or services to the specific academic department you're targeting. For example, companies that are interested in our engineering students provide products and resources for senior design projects or for competitions. Some companies suggest senior design ideas that the students complete on behalf of the company. These projects provide real-world marketplace applications for what is designed, created, and developed.

☐ You can invest in the Career Services office, but only after you're sure there will be a return on the investment. Many offices are eager to take your money with little commitment to use it for your benefit. One example that did work was a company that came to our campus and sponsored an event as we unleashed new campus software for running our on-campus recruiting program. We had water bottle gifts for students that were imprinted with the company's logo.

Communicate

One fundamental and timeless principle of recruiting is staying in touch with students on your radar screen. This means communicating with them. It sounds simple, but it's hard for busy recruiters to do. Students appreciate consistent and sincere communication. Even if the message is not profound or even positive, they want to be informed of what is happening on your side of the desk so that they can have a vision of their future. When students do not hear from recruiters or company contacts for long periods of time, they think the worst. While students need to take the initiative in communicating, the consistency and timeliness of your response is immeasurably important. The goal is to build a corporate presence on campus through relationships!

Final Thoughts

Recruiting on campus may not be for everyone, but if you consider recruiting or do recruit on campus, I encourage you to follow the tips that have worked so well on our campus. Developing deep relationships with the right campus can be a rich and rewarding experience. As your partnership grows, you'll see the career offices, the faculty, and the student body as an extension of your business. It's here that the next generation of professionals and leaders is being developed.

ACKNOWLEDGMENTS

I'd like to thank the wonderful people who helped make this ambitious dream of writing WHIM a reality. You all encouraged me as I plodded along, and many times you were more excited than I was about the project. I also thank God for the calling, opportunities, and gifts he has given me; I've tried to be a good steward of them.

A huge thanks to my amazing wife, Paula, and my children, Harrison, Davis, and Kate, who put up with my many nights away and the frequent distractions. Thanks for understanding! I also thank Adele Annesi, my editor and sounding board. It began with a providential call on a winter day, and the rest, as they say, is history. Thanks for joining me. My book is better because of you.

Thanks to my friends Mandy Alsposato and Erika Mayer in the Career Services Office at Grove City College. Jim Thrasher, your office inspired my hiring techniques and helped in the research for this book and the next. Thanks for agreeing to write the last chapter; I know many will find it helpful.

Special Thanks

A special thank-you goes to Len Garille; I learned everything from the master. Thanks for living the principles that I have tried to emulate in my career. Thank you to Mike Song for providing inspiration and guidance along the way.

A heartfelt thanks goes to all the folks who read the very rough, and I mean rough, drafts of the original WHIM, and who provided insights, comments, ideas, and direction to me: Jackie Biesedecki, Jack Burke, Vanessa Fernandez, David Fradkin, Russ Gasdia, Rick Goddard, Mike Kanz, Matt Kunzler, Noel Leuzarder, Frank Marcus, Victor Miller-brother (your insights and encouragement have been invaluable), Victor Miller-dad, Megan Montgomery, Ron Pearce, Ione Prawius, Nancy Rice, Charlie Smith, Chuck Sutton, and Ed Tavino.

A final thanks to those who read this book and visit WHIMuniversity.com. It is an honor that you would invest your time and energy reading and listening to what I have to say. I pray that you walk away with insights that will help you apply these principles to your professional and personal life.

About the Author
Garrett Miller is president and CEO of CoTria, A Productivity Training Company. He graduated from the University of Rhode Island and worked for a Fortune 50 pharmaceutical company for eighteen years, the last ten as a manager. After an award-winning career, Garrett began his venture as a business owner, author, keynote speaker, coach, and trainer. CoTria's clients include some of the world's greatest organizations. Garrett has been married twenty-seven years to his amazing wife, Paula, and is the proud father of three.

About the Contributor
Dr. Jim Thrasher was the Director of Career Services at Grove City College (GCC). Over twenty-five years, he developed a nationally recognized Career Services program. The Princeton Review has ranked GCC's career services office as one of the top twenty career services offices in the nation three times since the ranking's inception in 2008. He motivates students to pursue their calling, resulting in outstanding opportunities with national and international corporations. Dr. Thrasher now works as a Senior Fellow for Vocational Guidance at the college. Jim has been married for thirty years and is blessed with four wonderful children.

Resources
CoTria offers corporate and life-changing seminars:

WHIM Seminar Series:
- Hire on a WHIM: See why some of the greatest organizations in the world Hire on a WHIM. Build a low-maintenance, high-performance team by learning how to hire WHIM. Learn how to read resumes in a new way. Use the WHIM TimeLine™ as the forensic tool it's designed to be. Knowing which questions to ask and what to listen for are the keys to any interview. Learn why onboarding is the most important hour of an employee's tenure and why it is tied to retention.
- Character on a WHIM: This half-day seminar helps schools and parents learn how to instill the four must-have qualities in their students while the cement is still wet. Life is full of teachable moments, learn how to capitalize on them so impressions in their cement can be made and equip them with the WHIM foundation they need for success in life.
- Marriage on a WHIM: What does it take to have a successful marriage? The right foundation. Both individuals in a must-have Work Ethic, Humility, Integrity, and Humility before they commit to a life-long relationship. It takes a lot of each of these qualities to spend a life serving each other and building a relationship that grows and matures.
- Onboarding on a WHIM: This 90-minute seminar will help managers

and HR professionals understand how to make onboarding the most important hour of an employee's tenure. Proper onboarding will lead to better retention.

Productivity Series:
- Creating Space with Outlook® and Windows®: A 90-minutes seminar packed with the most useful time-saving tips and tricks. Understanding these powerful tools will revolutionize the way attendees handle email, calendars, tasks, and contacts.
- Creating Space with Mobile Office 365: This exciting 90-minute seminar demonstrates the power of Microsoft's amazing mobile app. Attendees will learn how to save time and energy and become more productive and responsive while mastering Mobile Office 365. Attendees will also learn mobile device best practices like performance-enhancing shortcuts, features, setting changes, apps, and navigation tips.
- Creating Space with Time and Technology: This 90-minute, fast-paced seminar will define what it means to protect and invest one's time. It begins by asking the most important question, the Big Why. Attendees will then learn how to use technology and time management techniques to make sure the answer to the Big Why can be achieved.
- Creating Space with OneNote®: This 60-minute course is dedicated to unlocking one of Microsoft's most powerful programs. Many technology users don't even realize they have access to this productivity tool. Attendees will learn how to incorporate OneNote into their daily lives. It is great for students, parents, professionals and is an ideal tool for collaboration.
- GetControl™ of Email: Cut email time by 20%. Reduce inbox clutter, prioritize tasks, and learn to write brilliant emails that are clear, concise, and actionable.
- GetControl™ of Meetings: Learn how to have fewer meetings, shorter meetings, and more productive meetings.
- GetControl™ and Get Organized: Develop a fast, powerful, and simple filing system so that you never lose an electronic file again.

For additional hiring information and resources, please visit:
CoTria.com and WHIMUniversity.com
Contact Garrett Miller
To reserve Garrett Miller as a trainer or keynote speaker, contact CoTria at 888-OnA-WHIM(662-9446), WHIMUniversity.com, or gm@WHIMUniversity.com

Also, from Garrett Miller:

Hired 'Right' Out of College – From Classes to Career: This step-by-step guide to discovering the career you were born to pursue is a must-read for all college and college-bound students. Hired Right will help students discover their natural aptitudes, talents, skills and abilities. Once this vital information is gathered then 'Right' helps them invest in areas that will confirm their gifts which will lead to promising direction. The reader will then learn how to develop a network that can serve as a valuable resource to make sure that they are hired 'Right' out of college.

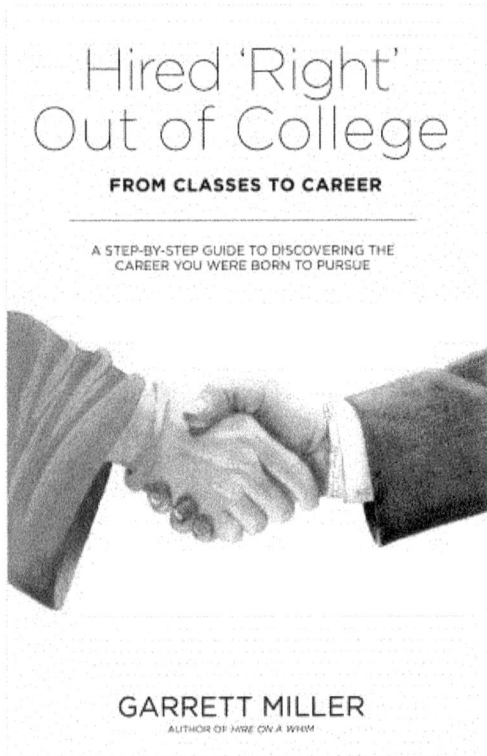

www.ingramcontent.com/pod-product-compliance
Lightning Source LLC
Chambersburg PA
CBHW020156200326
41521CB00006B/386